"JB"

Photo by FRIEDMAN-ABELES

J.B.

A PLAY IN VERSE

By Archibald MacLeish

The Pulitzer Prize Play, 1959

SAMUEL FRENCH, INC.
45 West 25th Street   NEW YORK 10010
7623 Sunset Boulevard HOLLYWOOD 90046
LONDON   TORONTO

Premiere: ANTA Theatre, New York City, Dec. 11, 1958

ALFRED DE LIAGRE, JR.

presents

ELIA KAZAN'S
production of

J.B.

by
ARCHIBALD MACLEISH

starring

PAT HINGLE   RAYMOND MASSEY
CHRISTOPHER PLUMMER

with
NAN MARTIN

Production Designed by   Costumes Designed by
Boris Aronson   Lucinda Ballard

Lighting by   Music by
Tharon Musser   David Amram

Associate Producer
Joseph I. Levine

Production Stage Manager
Robert Downing

CAST

ROUSTABOUTS ....*James Olson, Clifton James*
NICKLES ....*Christopher Plummer*
MR. ZUSS ....*Raymond Massey*
PROMPTER ....*Ford Rainey*
J.B. ....*Pat Hingle*
SARAH ....*Nan Martin*
DAVID ....*Arnold Merritt*
MARY ....*Ciri Jacobsen*
JONATHAN ....*Jeffrey Rowland*

3

RUTH	Candy Moore
REBECCA	Merry Martin
THE GIRL	Janet Ward
MRS. BOTTICELLI	Helen Waters
MRS. LESURE	Fay Sappington
MRS. ADAMS	Judith Lowry
MRS. MURPHY	Laura Pierpont
JOLLY	Lane Bradbury
BILDAD	Bert Conway
ZOPHAR	Ivor Francis
ELIPHAZ	Andreas Voutsinas

The Play is in Two Acts.

SCENE: *A traveling circus which has been on the roads of the world for a long time.*

MUSIC and SOUND EFFECTS

Music and sound effects are obtainable only on a tape. For full information write direct to Masque Sound & Recording Corporation, 331 West 51st Street, New York 19, N. Y.

The premiere performance of "J.B." by Archibald MacLeish was presented by the School of Drama, Yale University, at the University Theatre on April twenty-second, 1958. It was directed by F. Curtis Canfield, setting by Donald Oenslager, costumes and masks by Richard Casler, lighting by Joan Larkey, incidental music by Samuel Pottle. The cast: (as they speak)

MR. ZUSS MR. NICKLES	} circus vendors {	Ray Sader Bernard Engel
THE DISTANT VOICE		Russ Moro
SARAH, *J.B.'s wife*		Margaret Andrews
J.B.		James Shepherd
REBECCA RUTH MARY DAVID JONATHAN	} *J.B.'s children* {	Ann Satterthwait Suzanne Hull Janie Herndon James Inman Brandon Stoddard
First MAID		Judith Williams
SECOND MAID		Linda Robinson
FIRST MESSENGER		Ian Cadenhead
SECOND MESSENGER		William O'Brien
GIRL		Edith Lebok
BILDAD ZOPHAR ELIPHAZ	} *J.B.'s comforters* {	Richard Forsyth Joseph Hardy Fletcher Coleman
MRS. ADAMS		Bette Engel
JOLLY ADAMS		Janie Herndon
MRS. LESURE		Judith Williams
MRS. MURPHY		Edith Lebok
MRS. BOTTICELLI		Linda Robinson

J.B.

FOREWORD BY THE AUTHOR

(Reprinted from *The New York Times*)

A man may be forgiven for dramatizing an incident from the bible and even for modernizing it in the process. But what I have done is not so easy to excuse. I have constructed a modern play inside the ancient majesty of the Book of Job much as the Bedouins, thirty years ago, used to build within the towering ruins of Palmyra their shacks of gasoline tins roofed with fallen stones.

The Bedouins had the justification of necessity and I can think of nothing better for myself. When you are dealing with questions too large for you which, nevertheless, will not leave you alone, you are obliged to house them somewhere—and an old wall helps. Which is perhaps why so many modern plays have proved, on critical examination, to be reconstructions of the myths of Greece. That appeal to precedent, however, is of little use to me for my *J.B.* is not a reconstruction of the Book of Job— not, at least, a reconstruction of the kind presently familiar in which the discovery of the model is part of the adventure. My play is put in motion by two broken-down actors who believe, themselves, that the play *is* the Book of *Job* and that one of them is acting God and the other, Satan. When J.B. and his family appear however it is not out of the bible that they come.

But justification is still necessary and necessity is still the only justification I can plead. I badly needed an ancient structure in which to build the contemporary play which has haunted me for five years past and the structure of the poem of Job is the only one I know into which our modern history will fit. Job's search, like ours, was for the *meaning* of his afflictions—the loss of his children, the loss of everything he possessed, the loss of his wife's kindness, who turned upon him in his agony with those ineradicable words, surely the most dreadful ever spoken

6

by wife to husband: "Curse God and die!" There was no reason for all this: no reason the mind, at least, could grasp. Job was, by witness of God himself, and twice repeated, "a perfect and an upright man" and his destruction was, by the same unquestionable authority, "without cause." As for ourselves, there can be very few of us who are perfect, but the enormous, nameless disasters which have befallen whole cities, entire peoples, in two great wars and many small ones, have destroyed the innocent together with the guilty—and with no "cause" our minds can grasp.

We attribute these sufferings, except when it is we ourselves who have inflicted them, to the malevolence of our enemies, but even so we are appalled by all this anguish. Hiroshima, in its terrible retrospect, appalls us. And we attempt—millions of us, the psychiatrists say—to justify the inexplicable misery of the world by taking the guilt upon ourselves as Job attempted to take it: "Show me my guilt, O God." We even listen, as Job did, to the Comforters—though our Comforters are not like his. Where Job's Comforters undertook to persuade him, against the evidence of his own inner conviction, that he *was* guilty, ours attempt to persuade us that we are *not* —that we cannot be—that, for psychological reasons, or because everything is determined in advance by economic necessity anyway, or because we were damned before we started, guilt is impossible. Our Comforters are, if anything, less comfortable than Job's for they drive us from the last refuge in which our minds can hide from the enormous silence. If we cannot even be guilty then there are no reasons.

There are those, I know—because I have heard them —who will object that Job's story bears no true relationship to our own because God has changed in the interval. The God of Job is God the Creator of the Universe and science, they say, now knows that there is no such Creator—that the events of time progress by an automatism of their own—that the watch winds itself up and ticks by its own jiggling. The modern God of the scientific age, that is to say, does not control events: not, at least, events in the world of here and now.

I have no wish, and certainly no competence, to argue the questions of faith which underlie that attitude. But two things may be said from the merely human position. The first relates to the statement that science knows now there is no Creator. Does it? Einstein has told us that he had sometimes the sense that he was following, in his plumbings and probings of the universe, the track of an Intelligence far beyond the reaches of his own. The second thing to be said is this: that there has been nothing in human history which has brought mankind closer to the immanence of an infinite creativity than the revelation that the minutest particles of inert matter contain an almost immeasurable power. To me, a man committed to no creed, and more uncertain than I should be of certain ultimate beliefs, the God of Job seems closer to this generation than he has to any other in centuries.

*   *   *

My hero, called J.B. after the current fashion in business address, bears little relation, perhaps, to that ancient owner of camels and oxen and sheep. He is not a particularly devout man. But he is, at the beginning of the play, prosperous, powerful, possessed of a lovely wife, fine children—everything the heart of man can desire—and he is aware, as he could hardly help being, that God has made "an hedge about him and about his house and about all that he hath on every side." Not that the name of God is often in his mouth. He is one of those vastly successful American businessmen—not as numerous now as they were before the Great Depression—who, *having* everything, believe as a matter of course that they have a *right* to have everything. They do not believe this out of vulgarity. They are not Babbitts: on the contrary, they are most often men of exuberance, of high animal spirits, of force and warmth. They believe it because they possess in large measure that characteristically American courage, which has so often entertained Asian and European visitors, the courage to believe in themselves. Which means to believe in their lives. Which means, if their tongues can shape the words, to believe in God's goodness to them. They are not hypocritical. They do not think that they *deserve* more at God's hands than others. They merely think that they *have* more—and that they have a right to have it.

Such a man is no better prepared than Job was for the sudden and inexplicable loss of everything. And such a man must ask, as our time does ask, Job's repeated question. Job wants *justice* of the universe. He needs to know the reason for his wretchedness. And it is in those repeated cries of his that we hear most clearly our own voices. For our age is an age haunted and driven by the need to know. Not only is our science full of it but our arts also. And it is here, or so it seems to me, that our story and the story of Job come closest to each other. Job is not *answered* in the bible by the voice out of the whirling wind. He is *silenced* by it—silenced by some thirty or forty of the greatest lines in all literature—silenced by the might and majesty and magnificence of the creation. He is brought, not to *know,* but to *see.* As we also have been brought.

And what follows that *seeing* which cannot *know?* What follows is a chapter of the Book of Job which the theologians have tried again and again to explain away. Job is given all he had before twice over—all but his children who are the same in number but more beautiful. And that is not all. Not only is Job *given* his life again: Job *accepts* his life again. The man who was once highest and happiest and has now been brought lowest and made most miserable; the man who has suffered every loss, every agony, and for no reason, moral or intelligible, the mind can grasp; the man who has cried out to God for death, begged over and over to die, regretted the womb that bore him, yearned never to have been, never to have breathed the air or seen the light—*this* man accepts his life again, accepts to live his life again, take back his wife again, beget new children mortal as those others, risk himself upon the very hazard on which, before, his hopes were wrecked. And why? Because his sufferings have been justified? They have not been justified. God has merely lifted into the blazing fire of the imagination his own power and Job's impotence; his own immeasurable knowledge and Job's poor, trembling, ridiculous ignorance. Job accepts to live his life again in spite of all he knows of life, in spite of all he knows now of himself, because he loves life still in spite of life—*can* love it still.

Our own demand for justice and for reasons comes to the same unanswering answer. A few days before he died, the greatest of modern poets, and the most modern of great poets, William Butler Yeats, wrote to a friend that he had found what, all his life, he had been looking for. But when, in that letter, he went on to spell his answer out in words, it was not an answer made of words: it was an answer made of life: "When I try to put it all into a phrase I say, 'Man can embody truth but he cannot know it.' " Which means, to me at least, that man can *live* his truth, his deepest truth, but cannot speak it. It is for this reason that love becomes the ultimate human answer to the ultimate human question. Love, in *reason's* terms, answers nothing. We say that *Amor vincit omnia* but in truth love conquers nothing—certainly not death—certainly not chance. What love does is to affirm. It affirms the worth of life in spite of life. It affirms the wonder and the beauty of the human creature, mortal and insignificant and ignorant though he be: Even the mortal creature we ourselves have seen sitting on an earth reduced to ash-heap picking in agony at the cinders of a bomb-scorched skin. It answers life with life and so justifies that bravely tolling line of Shakespeare's which declares that love "bears it out even to the edge of doom." Love does: and for us no less than for that ancient man who took his life back after all that wretchedness.

J.B., like Job, covers his mouth with his hand; acquiesces in the vast indifference of the universe as all men must who truly face it; takes back his life again. In love. To live.

J.B.

ACT ONE

Interior, a traveling circus. The ring occupies L. C., *with its sidewalls broken* U. S. *and at* R. *and* L. *to permit entry from three ramps. Another ramp runs from* D. R. *to below the ring, giving onto the aisle of the theatre. Steps lead up to* D. L. *from this lower ramp. Tattered show banners frame the ramp leading off* L. *The* U. S. *ramp is reached by steps,* U. S., *and also by an upstage ramp that runs across the* U. R. *back of the set to* D. R. D. R , *steps lead up to a circus wardrobe, opening off a platform. Several tattered costumes hang in the wardrobe including a robe for* MR. ZUSS *and a fragmentary "devil's" costume for* NICKLES. *Concealed beneath these garments is a Godmask and a Satanmask. There is a small prop box at the* D. S. *end of the wardrobe. An arch of colored light globes curves above the entrance to the wardrobe. Above this, leading back over the* R. C. *side of the ring, more steps lead to a crow's nest half-way up a tent-pole— the sort of perch sometimes used by acrobats and wire-walkers. Beyond the ring, in a half-circle,* U. S., *the canvas of the backwall of the circus tent lies behind a low ground row. Ropes lead from this canvas into the flies. There are three rope lines,* D. R., *hanging loose. The backdrop shows an expanse of sky and horizon.*

The circus work lights are on when the audience enters the theatre. There is no act curtain. The banners, L., *are stirred by truant breezes. The stage is empty.*

11

A CIRCUS ROUSTABOUT *in khaki coveralls enters from* U. L., *above the banners. He carries two prop stools. He mounts the stairs* U. S., *places one stool in the ring,* R. *He carries the other stool to a position above the* D. R. *ramp, just outside the circus ring. He crosses* D. R., *sorts the loose lines, chooses one of them, which needs taping. He takes a roll of friction tape from his pocket, moves to a position just outside the ring,* D. R., *sits on the ramp, his feet resting on the lower ramp. He works on the end of the rope. Another* ROUSTABOUT, *dressed like the first, and smoking a cigar, enters* D. R., *moves* U. S., *along upper ramp. At the same time, a* PROP WOMAN, *wearing a khaki smock, enters* U. L., *above banners. She mounts steps, enters ring.* SECOND ROUSTABOUT *simultaneously, moves* D. S. *just outside ring. He crosses, and stands near* FIRST ROUSTABOUT, *puffing at his cigar; regarding audience idly. He pulls on his work gloves.*

PROP WOMAN, *at* C. *of ring, looks up at wrought-iron chandelier hanging over ring. At her glance, some of the globes in the chandelier light up. She moves slowly off on* L. *ramp, exiting between the banners.*

A PROP GIRL, *dressed like the* PROP WOMAN, *starts in from* U. L. *with a false table top. At the same moment, the* PROP WOMAN *returns, carrying a table over her head. She sets it on mark,* L. C., *in ring.* PROP GIRL *brings table top up steps, hands it to* PROP WOMAN, *returns down steps and off* U. L. PROP WOMAN *puts top on table, adjusts it.* GIRL *returns and commences piling seven prop stools at top of steps, making two or three trips off* L. *to accomplish this.* PROP WOMAN *commences setting stools around the table.* GIRL *joins her, sets the rest of the stools, then goes down steps, off* L.

While WOMEN *work, the* ROUSTABOUTS *belay the other*

two loose lines to large cleats set on floor below upper ramp at extreme R.

WOMAN *finishes setting stools.* GIRL *returns, carrying table cloth.*

> ### DIM HOUSE LIGHTS TO HALF.

GIRL *at* U. S. *end of table, hands one end cloth to* WOMAN. WOMAN, D. S., *tosses* D. S. *end of cloth carelessly over table, exits* L. *ramp.* GIRL *adjusts table cloth, exits* U. L. WOMAN *returns, carrying prop basket containing blue wine glasses and goblets, which she commences setting at the places on the table.*

> ### DIM HOUSE LIGHTS OUT.

WOMAN *finishes with the glasses, goes out* L. *ramp.* SECOND ROUSTABOUT *crosses to upper ramp, through ring.* GIRL *returns from* U. L. *and up steps, carrying a centerpiece of artificial fruit.*

The SHOW LIGHTS commence to build. CIRCUS CALLIOPE MUSIC is heard.

GIRL *places center piece on table, regards it happily.* WOMAN *returns from* L. *with dust cloth, which she and* GIRL *spread over table. Then they both exit down steps and out at* U. L., *the* GIRL *moving out ahead of the* WOMAN.

FIRST ROUSTABOUT *leans wearily on the lines,* D. R. SECOND ROUSTABOUT *calls to him from* U. S.

CALLIOPE MUSIC FADES A BIT UNDER DIALOGUE.

SECOND ROUSTABOUT.
  Hey—Rube!
FIRST ROUSTABOUT.
        What's the rush?

Can't even sleep on your feet in this business.
(*Crosses at* R. *of ring and joins* SECOND ROUSTABOUT.
SECOND ROUSTABOUT.
You do all right.
(*Regards canvas of tent, lying below him.*)
                    Goddam tent!
We sweat it up: they swat it down
Night after night after . . .
(ROUSTABOUTS *lean over, start pulling unseen ropes.
Tent backwall jerkily rises to marks—up full.*)
                    That does it! All set!

(SECOND ROUSTABOUT *flops onto his back behind the ring*
U. R. C. FIRST ROUSTABOUT *exits slowly to* L., *above the
banners, down steps and out.* NICKLES, *wearing a white
vendor's coat, and a comic mask, and carrying a tray of
popcorn in bags, runs down* L. *aisle of auditorium. He is
followed by* MR. ZUSS, *dressed in similar fashion, but
carrying a cluster of colored balloons. A blue balloon
tops the cluster.*)

NICKLES. (*At foot of aisle, regarding stage.*)
    This is it.
MR. ZUSS. (*Close behind him.*)
            This is what?
NICKLES.
    Where they play the play.

(NICKLES *moves up* L. *steps and into ring.* MR. ZUSS
crosses on lower ramp to R. *ramp.*)

MR. ZUSS. (*Faces* U. S.)
                    Bare stage?
NICKLES. (*Crosses through ring toward* D. R.)
    Heaven and earth! (*Points* R.) That platform's Heaven.
MR. ZUSS. (*Crosses* R. *Looks up at platform.*)
    Looks like Heaven.
NICKLES.
                    As you remember it?
MR. ZUSS.
    Somebody's got to. You weren't there.

Popcorn never sold in Heaven—
Not in my time.
               Where's the earth?
NICKLES.
Earth is where that table is.
(*Circles above table.*)
Here's where Job sits. At the table.
(*Crosses* R., *indicating platform.*)
God and Satan lean above.

(*Crosses to* L. *of* MR. ZUSS. *MUSIC fades away. Banners cease to stir.* MR. ZUSS *and* NICKLES *remove their comic masks, stow them in the pockets of their jackets.* MR. ZUSS *peers above, uneasily.*)

MR. ZUSS.
I wonder if we'd better, Nickles.
NICKLES.
Better what?
MR. ZUSS.
               Better play it.
NICKLES.
Why not? Who cares? We could show them!
The two best actors in America.
MR. ZUSS.
The *two* best actors?
NICKLES. (*Indicating the balloons.*)
               And now look at us!
Selling breath in bags!
MR. ZUSS. (*Indicating the bags of popcorn.*)
               And bags . . .
To butter breath with!
NICKLES.
               When they sell.
(*He unhooks the straps that hold his tray.*)
MR. ZUSS.
Merchandise not moving, Nickles?
NICKLES.
Moves wherever I do . . .

{Crosses U. S. *to* R. *to put tray under platform stairs.)*
      all of it.

MR. ZUSS. *(Puts down balloons,* R.)
      I wonder . . .

NICKLES. *(Moves into ring after putting down tray.)*
           Why not? Who cares? They don't.

MR. ZUSS.
      At least we're actors. They're not actors.
      They never acted anything.

NICKLES. *(Moving* C. *to above table.)*
      We could show them how it goes!
      Poor Job! That perfect creature,
      Crumpled on the dung of earth . . .

MR. ZUSS.
      Challenging *God!*

NICKLES.
           Crying to God!

MR. ZUSS.
      Demanding *justice!* Of God!

NICKLES.
              Imagine
      That! Asking God for justice!
      *(*NICKLES *removes his jacket, spreads it* D. C. *in ring.*
      MR. ZUSS *removes his jacket, puts it over his arm,* L.)*

      I heard upon his dry dung heap
      That man cry out who cannot sleep.
      "If God is God He is not Good.
      If God is good He is not . . ."

              Shall we
      Start? You'll play the part of . . .

MR. ZUSS.
              Naturally.

NICKLES.
      Naturally. And your mask?

MR. ZUSS.
           Mask!

NICKLES.
  Mask. Naturally. You wouldn't play God in your
  Face, would you?
MR. ZUSS.
                  What's the matter with it?
NICKLES. (*Crosses* R. *to* L. *of* MR. ZUSS.)
  God the Creator of the Universe?
  God who hung the world in time?
  You wouldn't hang the world in time
  With two-inch cat hair on your cutlets!

(MR. ZUSS *transfers jacket to his* R. *arm, looks out front,
majestically.*)

MR. ZUSS.
  WHATSOEVER IS UNDER THE WHOLE
  HEAVEN IS MINE!
NICKLES.
                  That's what I mean:
  You need a mask.
  (*Starts* L.)
MR. ZUSS.
                  Perhaps a more
  Accomplished actor . . .
NICKLES. (*Returns to* MR. ZUSS.)
                        Kiss your accomplishments!
  Nobody doubts your accomplishments—nobody.
  (*To audience.*)
  We remember Mr. Zuss:
  The one man for God in the theatre!
MR. ZUSS.
  You make me humble.
NICKLES.
                  No. I'm serious.
  The part was written for you.
MR. ZUSS. (*Self-deprecating gesture.*)
                        Oh!
NICKLES.
  But this is God in *Job* you're playing.
  God the Creator of the Universe—

Job's . . . *and* ours! Leviathan . . . Uranium . . .
You can't play HIM without a mask.
Human faces hide too much—too little.

MR. ZUSS.

What kind of mask?

NICKLES. (*Crosses into ring at* R. *side.*)
You'll find it somewhere.
Heaven's the great lost-and-found. Try Heaven!
(MR. ZUSS *starts up steps at* R. *to platform.* NICKLES
moves toward C. *in ring.*)
If God should laugh
The mare would calf
The cow would foal . . .

Diddle my soul.
(*He finishes* D. S. C.)

MR. ZUSS. (*On steps.*)
God never laughs! In the whole Bible!

NICKLES. (D. L. *below table, looking back at* MR. ZUSS.)
How *could* He laugh? He made it—
(MR. ZUSS *crosses to platform.*)
the toy
Top—the world—the dirty whirler!
(*Indicates expanse of ring, crosses* D. C. *to jacket.*)

MR. ZUSS. (*Jacket in* L. *hand. From platform.*)
What's so wrong with the world?

NICKLES.
Wrong with it!
Try to spin one on a dung-heap.
(*Kneels on jacket,* D. C.)
I heard upon his dry dung-heap
That man cry out who cannot sleep:
"If God is God He is not good,
If God is good He is not God; (*Rises.*)
Take the even, take the odd,
I would not sleep here if I could
Except for the little green leaves in the wood
And the wind on the water."

MR. ZUSS.

  You are a bitter boy.

NICKLES.

                 I taste of the world.
  I've licked the stick that beat my brains out—
  Stock that broke my father's bones. (*Lifts arms.*)

MR. ZUSS.

  I know. You've been around, you children!
  Our modern hero! Our Odysseus
  Sailing sidewalks toward the turd of
  Truth and touching it at last . . . in triumph!
  The honest, disillusioned—child!
  You sicken me!
  (*Puts jacket under robe hanging in wardrobe.*)

NICKLES.

                 All right. I sicken you.
  No need to be offensive, is there?
  (*Crosses to* D. S. *table.*)
  If you would rather someone else . . .

MR. ZUSS.

  Did what?

NICKLES.

            Played Job.

MR. ZUSS.

               Played Job?

NICKLES.

                   Nat-*u*-rally!
  (*Slaps table, crosses above table to* R. C. *of ring.*)
  Who else could play the part like me?
  (*Crosses* D. C. *toward jacket.*)
  God has killed his sons . . . his daughters . . .
  Taken his camels, oxen, sheep,
  Everything he has . . . and left him
  (*Falls to knees on jacket.*)
  Sick and stricken on a dung-heap—
  Not even the consciousness of crime to comfort him.

MR. ZUSS.

  Not Job. Not you. I wouldn't think of it.

NICKLES.

    You wouldn't think of me for Job?
    What would you think of?

MR. ZUSS.

                  Oh, there's always

    Someone playing Job.

NICKLES.

               There must be (*Rises.*)
    Thousands! What's that got to do with it?
    (*Crosses* U. R.)
    Millions and millions of mankind
    Burned, crushed, broken, mutilated,
    Slaughtered, and for what? For thinking!
    For walking round the world in the wrong
    Skin, the wrong-shaped noses, eyelids:
    Living at the wrong address—
    (*Crosses* D. *to jacket.*)
    London, Berlin, Hiroshima—
    Wrong night—wrong city.
    There never could have been so many
    Suffered more for less. But where do
    I come in? . . . Play the dung-heap?
    (*Crosses* L. *below table.*)

MR. ZUSS.

    All we have to do is start.
    Job will join us. Job will be there.

(MR. ZUSS *gets a robe from the wardrobe, puts it on.
Picks up* NICKLES' *Satan costume, conceals it in his* L.
hand. NICKLES *crosses to head of table.*)

NICKLES.

    I know. I know. I know. I've seen him.
    Job is everywhere we go,
    His children dead, his work for nothing,
    (*Sits* U.S. *stool, above table.*)
    Counting his losses, scraping his boils,
    Discussing himself with his friends and physicians,
    Questioning everything—the times, the stars.
    His own soul. God's providence.

(*Rises, crosses* R.)
What do *I* play?

MR. ZUSS.

What do you play?

NICKLES.

What do I play? You play God.
You play God and I play . . .

Ah!

MR. ZUSS.

I had assumed you knew.
(MR. ZUSS *tosses* SATAN *costume into ring. It falls at* NICKLES' *feet.* NICKLES *picks it up, gingerly. He drops it. Returns to his place at head of table. Sits.*)
I didn't mean to be nasty.
(*Waits for* NICKLES' *bus.*)

You see,
I think of you and me as . . . opposites.

NICKLES.

Nice of you.
(*Pause. Gives his costume a little kick.*)
Your opposite! A demanding role!

MR. ZUSS.

I know.

NICKLES. (*Rises.*)

But worthy of me. Worthy of me!
(*Picks up costume with toe of his shoe.*)

MR. ZUSS.

I have offended you. I didn't mean to.

NICKLES.

Did I say I was offended?

(MR. ZUSS *turns to the costume rack. His next speech, and* NICKLES' *speech, overlap.*)

MR. ZUSS. (*Examining the costumes.*)

Mask, he said. No mask . . . Costumes . . .
Vestures . . . centuries of vestures . . .
Prophets' mantles . . . High priests' ephods . . .
Copes . . . and surplices . . . and stoles . . .
(*Picks up Godmask and Satanmask. Back to audience.*)

NICKLES. (*Picks up Satan costume, adjusts it.*)
  So I play opposite to God!

  I heard upon his dry dung-heap
  That man cry out who cannot sleep:
  (*Addressing "JOB" in* U. S. *stool.*)
  "If God is God He is not good,
  If God is good He is not God;
  Take the even, take the odd,
  I would not sleep here if I could. . . ."
  (*Puts on costume.* NICKLES *crosses* D. S., *continues.*)
  "I would not sleep here if I could
  Except for the little green leaves in the wood
  And the wind on the water."
  (*Kicks white jacket off to* L. *side of stage.*)
  Show me the mask.
MR. ZUSS. (*Turning, masks concealed.*)
                          What mask?
NICKLES.

                                          My mask!
  You'll find it where the other was—in
  Heaven! (*To audience.*)
                    Father of lies they call me.
  Who knows enough to know they're lies?
MR. ZUSS. (*Lifts Godmask in* L. *hand.*)
  . . . *Justice* has a face like *this!*
  (*Puts mask before his face.*)
NICKLES.
  Like blinded eyes.
MR. ZUSS.
                          Like skies.
NICKLES.
                                          Of stone!
  Being magnificent and being right
  Don't go together in this universe.
  It's being wrong—a desperate stubbornness
  Fighting the inextinguishable stars—
  Excites imagination.
  (*Crosses* R. *to edge of ring.*)

Show me the
Other! Show me!

MR. ZUSS. (*Satanmask still concealed in his* R. *hand.*)
You won't find it
Beautiful, you understand.

NICKLES.

I know that:
Beauty's the Creator's bait!

MR. ZUSS. (*Holds mask out* D. S. R. *hand.*)
Well? That's it. You don't care for it?
It's not precisely the expression
Anyone would choose: I know that.
Evil is never very pretty—
Spitefulness either.
(NICKLES *crosses to below platform, reaches up.*)
Nevertheless it's
His: you'll grant that.

(NICKLES *takes his mask.*)

NICKLES. (*Holding mask to* R. *of his own face.*)
Evil you call it!
Look at those lips. They've tasted something
Bitter as a broth of blood
And spat the sup out. Was that evil?
Was it? Spitefulness you say—(*Crosses* L. *to table.*)
You call that grin of anguish spite?
Eyes that suffer: lips that spit—
I'd rather wear this ache of loathing
Night after night than wear that other
(MR. ZUSS *lifts his mask.*)
Once—that . . . white indifference! Horrible!
Horrible as a star above
A burning, murdered, broken city! (*Pause.*)
I'll play the part.

(MR. ZUSS *climbs to the crow's nest perch.*)

MR. ZUSS.

Put your mask on.

NICKLES. (*Crosses* D. L.)
　Give me the lines.

(*They put up masks before their faces.*)

DISTANT VOICE. (*From booth out front.*)
　　　　　　　　　WHENCE COMEST THOU?
(MR. ZUSS *and* NICKLES *lower masks.*)
NICKLES.
　Who said that? (*Masks up.*)
DISTANT VOICE.
　　　　　　WHENCE COMEST THOU?

(*Masks down.*)
MR. ZUSS.
　That was my line.
NICKLES.
　　　　　　　　Yes. . . . Who said it?

MR. ZUSS.
　He wants us to go *on*.
NICKLES.
　　　　　　　　Who does?

MR. ZUSS.
　Prompter probably. Prompter somewhere.
NICKLES. (*Shouting out front.*)
　Any . . . body . . . there? . . . (*Silence.*)
MR. ZUSS.
　　　　　　　　　Go on!

(*They raise their masks.*)

GODMASK.
　WHENCE COMEST THOU?

(*Silence. Masks down.*)

MR. ZUSS.
　　　　　　　　Go on!

NICKLES.
　　　　　　　　　What do I

　Say?

MR. ZUSS.

    It's in the Bible, isn't it?

NICKLES.

  I'm supposed to speak the Bible!

MR. ZUSS.

  Maybe that *Mask* of yours can speak it.

  Ought to know the lines by now.

(*Masks up.*)

GODMASK.

  WHENCE COMEST THOU?

SATANMASK. (*Offstage.*)

  FROM GOING TO AND FRO IN THE EARTH ...

  AND FROM WALKING UP AND DOWN IN

    IT ...

(SATANMASK *commences to laugh.* NICKLES *casts it to lower ramp. It continues laughing.*)

MR. ZUSS. (*Pulling off his mask.*)

  What's so funny? It's irreverent. It's blasphemous.

  (*LAUGH CUTS.*)

  After all, you are talking to God.

NICKLES.

  Do I look as though I'd laughed?

  If you had seen what I have seen

  You'd never laugh again ...

                    weep either.

  Those eyes see. They *see!*

(NICKLES *retrieves mask, crosses back to* D. L. *position.*)

MR. ZUSS.

                Now

  Listen! This is a simple scene.

  I play God. You play Satan.

  (FIRST *and* SECOND MAIDS *enter from* U. L., *up steps.*)

  God is asking where you've been.

  All you have to do is tell him.

  Simple as that.

  (MR. ZUSS *takes notice of them.*)

          "In the earth," you answer.

(FIRST MAID *crosses* D. S. *of table.* MAIDS *remove dust cloth, fold it.*)

NICKLES.

Satan answers.

MR. ZUSS.

All right—*Satan!*

(FIRST MAID *exits* U. L. *with cloth.* SECOND MAID *adjusts stool at head of table, crosses to* R. C. *in ring, faces* L. FIRST MAID *returns, stands* U. C.)

Let's get on. Let's play the play.

NICKLES.

You really think we're . . . playing?

MR. ZUSS.

Aren't we?

Somebody is. Satan maybe.
Maybe Satan's playing *you.*
Let's begin from the beginning.
Ready? (*Masks up.*)
Masks!

GODMASK.

WHENCE COMEST THOU?

SATANMASK.

FROM GOING TO AND FRO IN THE EARTH . . .
AND FROM WALKING UP AND DOWN IN IT.

(J.B. *enters from* L. *with his family:* REBECCA, *with* J.B. *Then* MARY *and* RUTH; SARAH, *the wife;* DAVID *and* JONATHAN. REBECCA *and* JONATHAN *carry bibs.* CHILDREN *take their places:* DAVID, RUTH *and* JONATHAN L. *of table;* MARY *and* REBECCA, R. J.B. *places* SARAH *at* D. S., *circles counterclockwise to head of table.* FIRST MAID *enters* U. L., *up steps. She stands* U. S. *of* 2ND MAID SATANMASK *speaks as they enter and move to their places.*)

GODMASK.

HAST THOU CONSIDERED MY SERVANT
JOB . . .
THAT THERE IS NONE LIKE HIM ON THE
EARTH.

A PERFECT AND AN UPRIGHT MAN . . . ONE
THAT FEARETH GOD AND ESCHEWETH EVIL.

SARAH.
  J.B. . . .

(*All the family bow their heads.* SARAH *puts* REBECCA'S
head down.)

J.B.
          Our Father which art in Heaven,
  Give us this day our daily bread.

FAMILY.
  Amenamen.
  (*All the family sit, except* SARAH.)
        Amen!
  (MAIDS *go out down steps and* U. L.)
        Amen!

SARAH.
  That was short and sweet, my darling.

J.B.
  What was?

SARAH.
        Grace was. (*Sits.*)

J.B.
          All the essentials.

SARAH.
  Give? Eat?

J.B.
        Besides they're hungry.

(*Affirmative ad-libs from* CHILDREN.)

SARAH.
  That's what grace is for—the hunger.
  Mouth and meat by grace amazed
  God upon my lips is praised.

(FIRST MAID *enters up steps from* U. L., *carrying a turkey on a platter.* J.B. *rises. She hands it to* J.B. *who sets
it.* SECOND MAID *follows at once with knife and carving
fork, which she gives to* J.B., *then* FIRST MAID, *seeing*

he needs a sharpener, exits U. L. *to get it. She returns*
with the sharpener, gives it to J.B., *exits* U. L.)

MARY.
Papá! Papá! He heard! He heard!
DAVID.
Who did?
RUTH.
                    Ourfatherwhichartinheaven.
J.B.
He did indeed. What a bird He sent us!
Cooked to a turn!
RUTH.
                    He heard! He heard!
JONATHAN. (*Flapping arms, jumping up and down in his*
place.)
He heard! He heard! He sent a bird!
SARAH.
That's enough now, children. Quiet!
Your father's counting.
J.B.
                    Not today.
Not this gobbler. Feed a regiment.
Nothing wrong with the food. *Or* the fixin's.
The day either—what's wrong with the day?
Tell me what day it is.
JONATHAN.
                    Turkey Day.
MARY.
Cranberry Day.
RUTH.
                    Succotash Day.
DAVID.
When we all can have white.

(J.B.*sharpens knife.* MR. ZUSS *crosses down to platform*
—sits on a box.)

JONATHAN.
                    And giblets to bite.

RUTH.
And two kinds of pie.
JONATHAN.

> And squash in your eye.

MARY.
And mashed potatoes with puddles of butter.
JONATHAN.
And gravy and such.
REBECCA. (*Rising.*)

> . . . and . . . and . . .

(*Breaks, darts to* SARAH. MR. ZUSS *crosses down to platform.* CHILDREN *scream with laughter.*)

SARAH. (*Her arms around* REBECCA.)
Children!
JONATHAN.

> And all eat too much.

SARAH.

> Children!

Quiet! Quiet every one of you.
(REBECCA *returns to her place, sits.*)
Answer your father's question, Jonathan.
Tell him what day it is.

(NICKLES *hangs his mask on* L. *tormentor, kicks white
jacket under banner,* D. L.)

JONATHAN.

> Thanksgiving.

SARAH.
What day is that?
JONATHAN.

> Thanksgiving Day.

DAVID.
The Day we give thanks to God.
MARY.

> For His goodness.

SARAH.
And did you, David? Did you, Mary?

Has any one of you thanked God?
Really thanked Him? Thanked Him for everything?
(*Rises, crosses to behind* DAVID.)
God doesn't give all this for nothing:
(MR. ZUSS *sits platform.*)
A good home, good food,
Father, mother, brothers, sisters.
(*Stands behind* RUTH.)
We too have our parts to play.
If we do our part He does His:
(*Ties on* JONATHAN'S *bib.*)
He always has. If we forget Him
He will forget. Forever. In everything.
David! Did you think of God?
(*She is back at her place.*)
Did you think when you woke in your beds this
  morning
Any one of you, of Him?

J.B. (*Referring to* DAVID.)
Of course he did. He couldn't have helped it.
(SARAH *sits, picks up* REBECCA'S *bib; draws* REBECCA
to her, and ties on the bib.)
Sweet Sal! Sweet Sal!
Children know the grace of God
Better than most of us. They see the world
The way the morning brings it back to them,
New and born and fresh and wonderful. . . .

SARAH.
Please, Job! I want the children
Somehow to understand this day, this
Feast. . . .

J.B.
                    Forgive me, Sal. I'm sorry. But they
Do. They understand. A little.
Look at me, all of you. Ruth, you answer.
Why do we eat all this—these dishes:
All this food? You say, Rebecca:
You're the littlest of us all.
Why?

REBECCA.
> Because it's good!

(*General laughter.*)

SARAH. (*Turning* REBECCA *to her.*)
> > Baby!
> Ah, my poor baby!

J.B.
> > Why your poor baby?
> She's right, isn't she? It is. It's good.

SARAH.
> Good—and *God* has sent it to us.

J.B.
> She knows that.

SARAH.
> > Does she? Job . . . do *you?*

NICKLES. (*Moves a bit* U. S., *to* MR. ZUSS.)
> What do *you* think? Think he knows?
> Think he knows what God can send him?

(MR. ZUSS *gestures* NICKLES *to* "*wait.*")

SARAH.
> Oh, I think you do . . . only . . .
> Times like this, when we're together . . .
> I get frightened, Job. . . . We have so
> Much.

J.B.
> > You ought to think I know.
> Even if no one else should, you should.
> Never since I learned to tell
> My shadow from my shirt, not once,
> Not for a watch-tick, have I doubted
> God was on my side—was helping me.

NICKLES. (*To audience.*)
> That's our pigeon!

J.B.
> > I've always known.
> Even young and poor I knew it.

People called it luck: it wasn't.
I never thought so from the first
Fine silver dollar to the last
Controlling interest in some company
I couldn't get—and got.
(FAMILY *laughs*.)

                  It isn't

Luck. (*Sits.*)

MARY.

      That's in the story.

JONATHAN.

                  Tell the

Story!

RUTH.

      Tell the lucky story!

REBECCA.

    Lucky, lucky, tell the lucky!

J.B. (*Rising*.)

    Tell the lucky? Tell the lucky.
Fellow came up to me once in a restaurant:
"J.B.," he says—I knew him . . .
"Why do you get the best of the rest of us?"
Fellow named Foley, I think, or Sullivan:
New-come man he was in town.

MARY.

    Your turn, Mother.

SARAH.

              Patrick Sullivan.

J.B. AND THE CHILDREN.

    Patrick Sullivan, that's the man!

J.B.

    "Why do you get the best of the rest of us?
I've got as many brains as you.
I work as hard. I keep the lamp lit.

J.B. AND THE CHILDREN.

    Luck! That's what it is," says Sullivan!

(NICKLES *crosses to above* L. *ramp entrance.*)

J.B.
"Look," I said, "Look out the window!
What do you see?" "The street," he tells me.
J.B. AND THE CHILDREN.
"The street," says I. "The street," says he.
J.B.
"What do you want me to call it?" he asks me.
"What do I want you to call it?" says I.
"A road," says I. "It's *going* somewhere."
"Where?" says he. "You say," I said to him.
J.B. AND THE CHILDREN.
"God knows!" says Mr. Sullivan!
J.B.
"He does," says I. "That's where it's going.
That's where I go, too. That's why."
"Why what?" says he. "I get the best of you
It's God's country, Mr. Sullivan."

(FAMILY *laughs*. NICKLES *crosses* D. L.)

J.B. AND THE CHILDREN.
"God forbid!" says Mr. Sullivan!
J.B.
I laughed till I choked. He only looked at me.
"Lucky so-and-so," he yells.
J.B. AND THE CHILDREN.
Poor Mr. Sullivan!
SARAH.
                    Poor Mr. Sullivan.
J.B.
It isn't luck when God is good to you:
It's something more. It's like those dizzy
Daft old lads who douse for water.
They feel the alder twig twist down
And know they've got it and they have:
They've got it. Blast the ledge and water
Gushes at you. And they knew.
It wasn't luck. They knew. They felt the
Gush go shuddering through their shoulders, huge

As some mysterious certainty of opulence.
They couldn't hold it. I can't hold it.
(J.B. *crosses* D. L. *side of table, carrying the two wine
glasses. As he passes below* SARAH, *he gives her a wine
glass. He crosses* R. C., *holding out a hand to* MARY *as
he passes below* REBECCA.)
I've always known that God was with me.
I've tried to show I knew it—not
Only in words.

SARAH.

Oh, you have,
I know you have. And it's ridiculous,
Childish, and I shouldn't be afraid. . . .
Not even now when suddenly everything
Fills to overflowing in me
(NICKLES *crosses* R. *a step.*)
Brimming the fulness till I feel
My happiness impending . . . like a danger.
If ever anyone deserved it, you do.

J.B.

That's not true. I don't deserve it.
It's not a question of deserving.

SARAH.

Oh, it is. That's all the question.
However could we sleep at night . . .

J.B. (D. C., *facing front.*)
Nobody *deserves* it, Sarah!—
Not the world that God has given us.
(NICKLES *crosses* D. S. *a step, watching* J.B.)
But I *believe* in it, Sal. I *trust* in it.
I trust my luck—my life—our life—
God's goodness to me.

SARAH.

Oh, I know.
I know you trust it. That's what frightens me.
It's not so simple as all that. It's not.
They mustn't think it is. God punishes.
God rewards and God can punish.
Us He has rewarded. Wonderfully.

    Kept us from harm, each one—each one.
    And why? Because of you—your . . . faithfulness.
J.B. (*Crosses to head of table.*)
    No. Because He's just. She's right.
    She's right, David. A man can count on Him.
    Look at the world, the order of it,
    The certainty of day's return. . . . (*Lifting glass.*)
    To be . . . become . . . and end—are beautiful.
    Trust our luck, my Sal! Trust in it!

(J.B. *sits.* FAMILY *freezes positions.*)

NICKLES.
    Trust in our luck! Our *life! Trust* in it!
MR. ZUSS. (*Rises.*)
    You don't like him.
NICKLES.
                I don't have to.
    You're the one that has to like him. . . .
    (*Crosses to* L. *entrance.*)
    The love of life! The *love* of *life!*
    (*Crosses to* L. *of* DAVID.)
    Poisoning their little minds
    With love of life! At that age!
MR. ZUSS.
                   No,
    I thought he made that small familiar
    Feast a true Thanksgiving. Only . . .
NICKLES. (*Crosses to* R. *of* J.B.)
    Thanksgiving for what? For whom? For when?
    (*Whisper to* J.B.)
    The best thing you can teach your children
    Next to never drawing breath
    Is choking on it!
    (*To* MR. ZUSS.)
              Only what?
MR. ZUSS.
    Only . . . I wonder if he knows.

NICKLES.
  Knows what?
MR. ZUSS.

                    Knows he's . . . in it.

NICKLES.

                                   In it?

MR. ZUSS.
  He has the wealth, the wife, the children . . .
  Position in the world.
NICKLES.

                    The piety?

MR. ZUSS.
  He loves God, if that's what you're saying.
NICKLES.
  Piety's hard enough to take
  Among the poor who *have* to practise it.
MR. ZUSS.
  This man *has* his—and he's grateful.
NICKLES.
  Bought and paid for like a waiter's smirk.
  (*Crosses* L. *of* J.B.)
  You know what talks when that man's talking?
  All that gravy on his plate—
  His cash—his pretty wife—his children.
  Wait till you lift the lot—he'll sing
  Another canticle—to different music.

(*Crosses* U. L. *to* L. *entrance.* J.B. *and* REBECCA *commence
singing the "Family Song."* J.B. *rises.* REBECCA *leaps
into his arms. He moves* D. S. *and sits in her place, holding* REBECCA *in his lap.* JONATHAN *moves* D. L. *to* L.
of SARAH. RUTH *stands slightly to* L. *of* JONATHAN.
DAVID *moves to behind this group.* MARY *remains in
her place. As the song starts,* MAIDS *enter* U. L. FIRST
MAID *removes turkey, takes it off* U. L. SECOND MAID
strikes off carving set. MAIDS *return. The* FIRST *with a
tray on which she and* SECOND MAID *put glasses.* FIRST
MAID *exits with tray,* SECOND *with fruit.*)

(BEHIND THE TENT BACKWALL, FIRE DROP IS LOWERED. HORIZON DROP IS FLOWN.)

J.B. AND REBECCA. *(Singing.)*
    I love Monday . . . Tuesday . . . Wednesday . . .
    Where have Monday, Tuesday gone?
REST OF FAMILY. *(Singing.)*
    Under the grass tree,
    Under the green tree,
    One by one.

    I love Monday, Tuesday, Wednesday,
    Where have Monday, Tuesday gone?
    Under the grass tree,
    Under the green tree,
    One by one.

(REBECCA and RUTH join hands, face J.B. and sing together.)

REBECCA AND RUTH. *(Singing.)*
    Caught as we are in Heaven's quandary
    Is it we or they are gone
    Under the grass tree,
    Under the green tree,
    One by one?

(FAMILY repeats song, and they exit L.: JONATHAN, followed by DAVID; SARAH moving to L. entrance, and looking back at J.B. as REBECCA and RUTH exit below her, out L., and MARY crosses above table, and out L., passing below SARAH. MR. ZUSS crosses up to perch. SARAH exits L.)

FAMILY. *(Singing as they exit.)*
    Caught as we are in Heaven's quandary
    Is it we or they are gone
    Under the grass tree,
    Under the green tree,
    One by one?
    (Offstage, they continue singing.)

I love Monday, Tuesday, Wednesday . . .
One by one.
J.B. (*Rises, crosses to head of table—speaks.*)
I love Monday, Tuesday, Wednesday . . .

(*Exits* L. FIRST MAID *enters* U. L., *takes two* R. *stools to*
R. C., *places them together on mark; sets* U. S. *stool to*
U. S. *position.* SECOND MAID *strikes* D. S. *stool Offstage*
U. L. FIRST MAID *then strikes* U. S. *stool and* L. C. *stool*
to Off U. L.)

NICKLES.
God will teach him better, won't He?
God will show him what the world is—
What a man is! The ignoble creature—
Victim of the spinning joke!
MR. ZUSS.
Teach him better than he knows!—
God will show him God—what God *is:*
Enormous pattern of the steep of stars,
Minute perfection of the frozen crystal,
Inimitable architecture of the slow,
Cold, silent, ignorant sea-snail:
The unimaginable will of stone:
Infinite mind in midge of matter!

(SARAH *enters from* L., *crosses to* D. R. C. J.B. *follows,*
removes his coat, puts it over SARAH'S *shoulders.*)

(*SOUND OF DISTANT CHURCH BELLS.*)

NICKLES.
Infinite mush! Wait till your pigeon
Pecks at the world the way the rest do—
Eager beak to naked bum!
MR. ZUSS.
You ought to have your tongue torn out!
NICKLES.
All men should: to suffer silently.
MR. ZUSS.
Nothing this good man might suffer,

Nothing at all would make him yelp
As you do. He'd praise God no matter.
NICKLES.
Why must he suffer then?
MR. ZUSS.

                              To praise!
NICKLES. (*Crosses* D. S. L.)
He praises now. Like a canary.

Shall I tell you why?
(*Crosses into lower ramp.*)
                              To *learn!*
Every human creature born
Is born into the bright delusion
Beauty and loving-kindness care for him.
Suffering teaches! Suffering's *good* for us!
Imagine men and women dying
Still believing that the cuddling arms
Enclosed them!
(J.B. *kisses* SARAH.)
                              They would find the worms
Peculiar nurses, wouldn't they? Wouldn't they?
(J.B. *and* SARAH *exit* L., *his arm around her.*)
(*Sings "Devil Theme."*)
What once was cuddled must learn to kiss
The cold worm's mouth: that's all the mystery.
That's the whole muddle.
(*Speaks.*)
Well, we learn it.
God is merciful and we learn it.
We learn to wish we'd never lived.

(*Crosses* R. *to* R. *ramp entrance of ring.* MAIDS *enter from*
U. L. FIRST MAID *crosses to below table,* SECOND *to*
above. They strike table, with cloth, off L. *entrance,*
through banners. SECOND ROUSTABOUT *rouses, puts feet*
up on ring, U. S.)

MR. ZUSS.
He'll never learn that lesson. Never.

NICKLES. (*Crosses above table.*)
Won't he? When the anguish starts?

(FIRST ROUSTABOUT *enters from* U. L., *up steps, crosses
to* U. S. C., *kicks* SECOND ROUSTABOUT *on the foot.*)

FIRST ROUSTABOUT.
Here we go.

(*He goes to position behind platform* R. *to change into
soldier outfit.* SECOND ROUSTABOUT *rises, follows him.*
FIRST ROUSTABOUT *picks up balloons,* D. R., *hands them
Offstage,* D. R. ROUSTABOUTS *change into soldier attire,
stand at ease on upper ramp,* D. R.)

NICKLES.
                    Here we go.
      (*Sits on stool above table.*)
Shall I tell you how it ends?
Shall I prophesy? I see our
Smug world-master on his dung-heap,
Naked, miserable, and alone,
Pissing the stars. Ridiculous gesture!—
Nevertheless a gesture—meaning
All there is on earth to mean:
Man's last word . . . and worthy of him!
MR. ZUSS.
He'll trust the will of God no matter.
NICKLES.
Why try the trust then?
MR. ZUSS.
                              Why? To see!

NICKLES.
See . . . *what?*
MR. ZUSS.
                    See . . . God!
NICKLES.
A fine sight from an ash heap, certainly.
MR. ZUSS.
It's from the ash heap God is seen

Always! Always from the ashes.
Every saint and martyr knew that.

(*RUSH OF WIND.* Mr. Zuss *unhooks mask.*)

Distant Voice.
HAST THOU CONSIDERED MY SERVANT,
JOB . . .

(Nickles *rises, moves* u. s. *stool to* u. l. *of table. Crosses
to* l. *tormentor, puts mask before his face.*)

Godmask.
HAST THOU CONSIDERED MY SERVANT JOB
THAT THERE IS NONE LIKE HIM ON THE
EARTH,
A PERFECT AND AN UPRIGHT MAN, ONE
THAT FEARETH GOD AND ESCHEWETH
EVIL?
Satanmask.
DOTH JOB FEAR GOD FOR NAUGHT?
HAST THOU NOT MADE AN HEDGE ABOUT
HIM
AND ABOUT HIS HOUSE
AND ABOUT ALL THAT HE HATH ON EVERY
SIDE?
THOU HAST BLESSED THE WORK OF HIS
HANDS
AND HIS SUBSTANCE IS INCREASED.
BUT PUT FORTH THINE HAND NOW AND
TOUCH
ALL THAT HE HATH . . . AND HE WILL
CURSE THEE TO THY FACE!
Godmask.
BEHOLD!
ALL THAT HE HATH IS IN THY POWER!
Distant Voice.
ONLY . . . UPON HIMSELF . . . PUT NOT
FORTH THY HAND!

GODMASK.
ONLY . . . UPON HIMSELF . . . PUT NOT
FORTH THY HAND!

(MR. ZUSS *hangs up mask. THERE IS A BURST OF BAND MUSIC.* SOLDIERS *start* U. S. C. *on upper ramp. From* R. *onto lower ramp, there enters a one-legged* SOLDIER, *on a crutch, bearing aloft a newspaper with headlines: WAR ENDS. He shouts, repeatedly: "It's over! It's over!" He is accompanied by a* PREACHER, *with a tambourine. The two dance a wild fandango together in this area.* TWO SAILORS *and* TWO WAVES, *in whites, race on from* R. *to positions under* R. *platform, and embrace wildly. Then they rush back off* R., *followed by one-legged* SOLDIER *and* PREACHER. SARAH *enters from* L. *through banners, to* U. C. *in ring, carrying needlepoint. She pushes imaginary curtains aside, looks* U. S. *at* SOLDIERS. *J.B. enters* L., *carrying two glasses and decanter, which he sets on table from* L. *side. He puffs contentedly at cigar.*)

(*MUSIC UNDER DIALOGUE.*)

SARAH.
Look, Job! Look! Across the street.
Two soldiers.
J.B. (*Enters to* L. *of table. Putting glasses and bottle on table.*)
What about them?
SARAH.
Only they
Stare so.

(FIRST SOLDIER *moves to* U. C. *entrance to ring.* SECOND SOLDIER *weaves, drunkenly, a bit to his* R., *on upper ramp.*)

J.B.
Stare at what?
SARAH.
The house.

I think they're drunk. . . . A little.

(MR. ZUSS *crosses down to platform* D. S. *end.*)

J.B. (*Affably.*)

                                    Plastered!

SARAH.
One of them anyway.
(*Crosses* D. R. C., *sits on* L. *stool.*)
                                    He wobbles.

J.B.
That's no wobble. That's a waltz step.

(FIRST SOLDIER *rings imaginary DOORBELL, which sounds, off* L. *MUSIC CUTS.*)

SARAH.
They're at the door.

J.B. (*Crosses* R. *with drinks.*)
                                    They sure are.

SARAH.
What do you think they . . .

J.B. (*Crosses* R. C. *above* SARAH, *hands her a drink, sits* R. *stool.*)
                                    I don't know.

SARAH.
What do you think they want, two soldiers?

J.B.
No idea. Johnson will tend to them.

(NICKLES *looks off* L.—*presumably for "Johnson."*)

SARAH. (*Looking at the* SOLDIERS.)
I've never seen such staring eyes.

J.B.
Glazed. Just glazed.

SARAH.
                        I know, Job.
They have some kind of message for us.
David has sent them with a message—
Something about his regiment. They're coming

Every day now, ship by ship.
I hear them in the harbor coming.
He couldn't write and so he sent them.

(FIRST SOLDIER *gestures to* SECOND SOLDIER *to roll down his sleeves and button them.* SECOND SOLDIER *does so.*)

J.B.
Pretty drunk for messengers, those soldiers.
SARAH.
What does it matter?
(*Folds needlepoint, hands glass to* J.B. FIRST SOLDIER *rings bell.*)   They're just boys.
They've just got home. It doesn't matter.
J.B.
Johnson's a judge of drunks. He'll handle them.

(NICKLES *crosses* U. L. *to* U. S. *steps, above* SOLDIERS.)

SARAH. (*Rises, crosses* L., *puts needlepoint on table.*)
He mustn't send them off. Don't let him!
NICKLES. (*Affecting "Johnson's" voice.*)
Two young . . . gentlemen to see you.
Friends, they say, of Mr. David.
SARAH. (*Crosses to behind stools,* R. C.)
Oh, I knew! I knew! I knew!

(J.B. *rises, crosses* L. C., *puts glasses on table, crosses* U. C. *to* L. *of* U. C. *entrance.*)

J.B. (*Shaking hands with* FIRST SOLDIER.)
Come in, gentlemen. Come in. Come in.
David's friends are always welcome.
This is David's mother.

(FIRST SOLDIER *removes cap, and tentatively shakes hands with* SARAH. SECOND SOLDIER *sways to position* D. R. *of* SARAH, *crossing above her.*)

SARAH.
                    Won't you sit

Down?

FIRST SOLDIER. (*Crosses* D. R., *sits* L. *stool.*)
        What did I tell you, Punk!
Any friends of David's.

(J.B. *places stool below table—from* L. *of table for*
SARAH.)

SARAH. (*At his* L.)
                There.
  Sit down.
FIRST SOLDIER.
        It's just, we saw the number.
SARAH.
  And David asked you to drop in.
FIRST SOLDIER.
  Any friend of his, he told us.
  Any time.
SECOND SOLDIER.
        And we were cold:
  A cold, hard march. . . .
FIRST SOLDIER. (*Pulls* SECOND SOLDIER *down to* R. *stool,*
takes off SECOND SOLDIER'S *cap, hands it to him.*)
                What the
  Hell's the matter with *you!* You drunk?
SARAH.
  Sit by the fire, both of you. Where was he?

(SOLDIERS *hunch forward a bit, as if drawing nearer to*
a fireplace. SARAH *crosses to below table.*)

FIRST SOLDIER.
  Where was who?
SARAH. (*Sits below table.*)
           David.
FIRST SOLDIER.
          When?
J.B.
  When he told you. (*He whispers to* SARAH.)
SECOND SOLDIER.
        In the mess.

FIRST SOLDIER.
  Any friends of his, he told us.
  Any time at all . . . Why?
  (J.B. *crosses to* L. *entrance.*)
  You think we're lying to you?
J.B. (*Turning back.*)

  Certainly

  Not. (*Exits* L.)
FIRST SOLDIER.
      You think we never knew him?
SARAH.
  Of course you did. You *do*.
FIRST SOLDIER.

          We knew him.

SECOND SOLDIER.
  Fumbling among the faces . . .
FIRST SOLDIER.

              Will you shut
  Up, or will I clout you, Big Mouth? (*To* SARAH.)
  That's why we come; because we knew him.
SECOND SOLDIER.
  To tell you how we knew him.
SARAH.

            Thank you.

SECOND SOLDIER.
  How it was with him. . . .
FIRST SOLDIER.

            Listen, Punk!

SECOND SOLDIER.
  How, by night, by chance, darkling . . .
  By the dark of chance . . .
FIRST SOLDIER.

          He's drunk.

SECOND SOLDIER.
  The war done . . . the guns silent . . .
  No one knows who gave the order.
FIRST SOLDIER. (*Rises.*)
  Like I say, because he said to.

Any friend of his he said to.
Just to tell you we knew David.

(J.B. *returns with two more glasses, stands* L. *of table.*)

SECOND SOLDIER.
Maybe drink to David maybe . . .
SARAH. (*Rises.*)
Yes! Oh, yes! Let's drink to David.
(*She crosses* U. R. C. *to get extra footstool.*)
J.B.!
J.B.
Bourbon? Scotch?

(FIRST SOLDIER *crosses to* R. *of table, accepts drinks from*
J.B., *crosses* R., *gives glass to* SECOND SOLDIER, *sits.*)

FIRST SOLDIER.
                    Now you're
Cooking!
SARAH. (*Placing stool before* FIRST SOLDIER.)
            That's right. Put your feet up.
(FIRST SOLDIER *hesitates.*)
Oh, they're not too dirty. David's are
Dirtier. I'm sure of that.
SECOND SOLDIER.
David's feet!

(SARAH *crosses* L. *to* J.B., *he gives her a drink.*)

FIRST SOLDIER.
            I'll say they are.
(*Awkward pause.*)
Look! What's going on here: David's
Feet!
SARAH.
            I meant—with all that marching.
(*Looks at* J.B., *sits below table.*)
FIRST SOLDIER. (*Placing drink on stool before him.*)
I don't get it. Look, it's true—
They didn't have the right length lumber:
(MR. ZUSS *starts up ladder toward perch.*)
We did the best we could. . . .

(J.B. *puts down glass, stands behind* SARAH. MR. ZUSS *unhooks mask and drumstick.*)

J.B.
                                                    What in
God's name are you saying, Soldier?
SARAH.
What does he mean, the lumber?

(NICKLES *crosses* D. L.)

FIRST SOLDIER.
                                          You don't
Know?
    (*To* SECOND SOLDIER.)
            Ain't that the army for you!
They don't know. They never told them.
SARAH.
Told us what?
FIRST SOLDIER. (*Rises, crosses* U. C.)
                    We better go.

(SECOND SOLDIER *puts drink on stool beside* FIRST SOL-DIER'S *drink.* SARAH *looks at him.* NICKLES *watches from the first step,* D. L.)

SARAII.
No! Please! Please! No!

(*Crosses* U. R. *to* FIRST SOLDIER. J.B. *crosses* U. S. *to* L. *of* FIRST SOLDIER. MAIDS *enter from* U. L., *stand on* U. S. *steps.*)

FIRST SOLDIER.
Come on, we're getting out, you lunkhead.
J.B. (*As if to halt* FIRST SOLDIER.)
Not until you've told me. Sarah!
Perhaps you'd better, Sarah. . . .
SARAH.
                                          Please,
I want to hear it.

First Soldier.

Jesús! . . . Jesús! . . .

(First Soldier *brushes past* J.B. *and* Sarah *onto ramp,*
U. S., *facing* R.)

Sarah.
What is it we were never told?

(J.B. *and* Sarah *cross to* R. *of table.*)

Mr. Zuss. (*On perch.*)
Ready?
Nickles.
Got to be, don't they? Got no
Choice. Disasters . . . agonies . . .
Mr. Zuss.

I meant

You.
Sarah. (*Overlapping other speeches.*)
David is our son . . . our son . . .

(Mr. Zuss *lifts a drumstick, and his mask. He brings
down the drumstick. Off* R., *DRUM BEAT. Holds onto
them. MUSIC UNDER DIALOGUE.* Second Soldier
rises, wobbly on his pins, looks at Sarah, *crosses* D. L. C.
to edge of ring.)

(*MUSIC DIMS HALF POINT: PLAYS TO END OF
TUNE.*)

J.B. (*Crosses to* R. *of* Second Soldier.)
It isn't true . . . It isn't possible . . .
We had a letter from him. . . . After the
End of it. . . . We had a letter . . .
Second Soldier.
What shall I say to you? What I saw?
What I believe I saw? Or what
I must have seen . . . and have forgotten.
Nickles. (*At* D. L. *front.*)
Can't be happening to us. It can't be.

J.B.
   David's all right. He is. He has to be.
NICKLES.
   God won't let it happen. Not to
   Job, the perfect and the upright man.
J.B.
   I know he is. The war is over.
NICKLES.
   Job *deserves* his luck. He's earned it.
J.B.
   It never could have happened. Never.
   Never in this world.
NICKLES.
                   This world! This world!
   Suppose it did though—suppose it did!
   What would this world be made of then?

(SARAH *crosses to* R. *of* SECOND SOLDIER.)

SARAH. (*Touches* SOLDIER'S *face.*)
   David's all right. I know he is.
SECOND SOLDIER.
   I ONLY AM ESCAPED ALONE TO TELL THEE.

(SECOND SOLDIER *waves to* U. C. *entrance, then crosses*
D. C. *to* R. *of* J.B. SOLDIER *starts to speak, cannot. He*
goes out U. S. C. *to ramp to join* FIRST SOLDIER.)

SARAH.
   Job! He's dead! God has taken him!

(*Exits* L. MR. ZUSS *lifts mask.*)

J.B.
   We had a *letter*. After the end of it. . . .

(SARAH *sobs, off* L. J.B. *hurries out after her.* FIRST
MAID *crosses to* D. R. *stools, sets glasses from footstool*
on table. SECOND MAID *crosses to table with tray; strikes*
glasses, bottle and needlepoint. Exits U. L., *down steps.*
FIRST MAID *takes away two stools* D. R. *that have formed*
seats during scene, leaving the "footstool" only. She exits

U. L., *down steps.* MR. ZUSS *hangs up mask and crosses to platform.* SOLDIERS *move* R. *on* U. S. *ramp.*)

NICKLES. (*Moving to lower ramp,* D. C.)
Even a perfect and an upright man,
Teach him long enough, might learn!

(NICKLES *hums "bop" phases to "Devil Theme" and crosses* U. R. *ramp and steps through ring to under perch.* PROP WOMAN *has entered from* U. L. *and stands below steps, holding prop camera aloft.*)

MR. ZUSS.
Learn . . . what?

(NICKLES *continues "Scat" vocal, runs* U. S. *Takes camera from* PROP WOMAN, *who exits* U. L.)

NICKLES.
Your providence!
(*Tosses camera to* FIRST REPORTER, *on ramp.*)
MR. ZUSS.
Keep your
Tongue in your teeth!

(*A BURST OF JAZZ MUSIC. Three couples hurry in from* D. R. *to positions under the platform,* R., *and dance, provocatively, the girls with their behinds wiggling* D. S. *"*THE GIRL*" is nearest* C. NICKLES, U. S. C., *ushers* FIRST REPORTER *into ring.* SECOND REPORTER *follows.* NICKLES *crosses* D. R., *cuts in on* THE GIRL *and her partner. When this happens, other couples "freeze."* SECOND REPORTER *crosses* L. *to* D. L. *near edge of ring.* NICKLES *dances with* THE GIRL *on* D. R. *ramp. She pushes him away. Her wrap has fallen to the floor.* NICKLES *gets it.*)

GIRL.
I don't like it.
NICKLES. (*At* R. *of* GIRL, *putting wrap on her shoulders.*)
You'll do fine.

GIRL.

I don't like it.
I wish I was home in bed with a good
Boy . . . or something. I don't like it.

FIRST REPORTER. (*Crosses* D. R. C., *camera in* L. *hand.*)
You'll do fine.

GIRL.

I won't do fine:
I'm frightened.

FIRST REPORTER. (*Grabs* GIRL *by* L. *hand.*)
All you do, you go up to them,
Get them talking, keep them looking . . .

GIRL.
Go up to them yourselves, why don't you?

FIRST REPORTER.
Sure, and get the brush off.
(*Pushes* GIRL *to* C. *in ring, below him.*)
Girl like
You can keep them talking: keep them
Looking, that is. (*Slaps* GIRL *on the rump.*)
Pretty girl!

GIRL.
All I know is I don't like it.
Keep them talking till a flash bulb
Smacks them naked in the face—
It's horrible!

FIRST REPORTER.
It's genius! Listen, lady!
How do I get the photograph without?
Answer me that. How do I get the
Look a mother's face has maybe
Once in a lifetime: just before
Her mouth knows, when her eyes are knowing?

GIRL.
I can't do it.

FIRST REPORTER.
She can't do it.
All you got to do is walk.
Wiggle your can. Keep them looking.

Then he tells them. Then I take them.
Then you beat it. Then that's that—
Except the drink we're going to buy you
Payday evening if you're good—
And if you're not there's lots of liars.
SECOND REPORTER.
     You don't have to tell them: I do.
GIRL.
     Why do *you?*
SECOND REPORTER.
              Because I have to.
There's always someone has to—someone
Chosen by the chance of seeing,
By the accident of sight—
Having witnessed, having seen . . .
He only . . .
FIRST REPORTER.
              He was there. He has to.
Route Two. Under the viaduct.
Travelling seventy—seventy-five.
Kid was driving them was drunk.
Had to be drunk. Just drove into it.
He was walking home. He saw it.
Saw it start to. Saw it had to.
Saw it happen. J.B.'s son.
J.B.'s daughter. Four in all.
All of the four of them just kids
Screaming when they hit the wall.
     (*Crosses* U. C.)
SECOND REPORTER.
     Then silent . . .
     (MR. ZUSS *turns* U. S.)
                    Blond in all that blood . . .

(MR ZUSS *crosses to perch, unhooks mask and* .*. um-
stick. CAR SOUND, off* R.)

GIRL.
     He can't tell them *that!*

FIRST REPORTER.

He has to.

Someone has to.

(*CLICK OF CAR DOOR, off* R.)

(*Hears car, crosses* U. S. *to entrance.*)

They don't know.

They've been out all evening somewhere.

(NICKLES *crosses to* R. *entrance.* GIRL *crosses to* R. C. *in ring, beneath perch.*)

FIRST REPORTER. (*Getting out a cigarette.*)

That's them. They're coming. Quiet!

GIRL.

I can't do it!

FIRST REPORTER. (*Savagely, crosses to* GIRL, *who cowers.*)

You can do it!

(FIRST REPORTER *thrusts cigarette into* GIRL'S *mouth, then crosses to* L. *of table, facing* D. SECOND REPORTER *has his foot on the rim of the ring* D. L. SARAH *and* J.B. *enter from* R., *along upper ramp, in formal attire.* NICKLES *crosses* L. *outside ring to above* C. *entrance.*)

SECOND REPORTER.

I who have understood nothing . . . have known

Nothing . . . have been answered nothing . . .

I ONLY AM ESCAPED ALONE. . . .

(J.B. *and* SARAH *laugh together, and enter ring,* U. C. GIRL *goes to below them, facing* U. S.)

GIRL.

Good

Evening. What a pleasant evening.

Back from the theatre so soon?

We're neighbors, don't you know? You've met my

Miffkin walking me each morning. . . .

You know Muff, my purple poodle. . . .

Isn't it a pleasant evening?

(J.B. *crosses* D. L. *to* SECOND REPORTER.)

SECOND REPORTER.
  I'm from the press. There's been an accident . . .

(MR. ZUSS *raises and lowers the drumstick. DRUM BEAT off* R. *Hangs up stick.*)

FIRST REPORTER. (*Crosses to* L. *of* SARAH.)
  Four kids in a car. They're dead.
  Two were yours. Your son. Your daughter.
  Cops have got them in a cab.
  Any minute now they'll be here!

(FIRST REPORTER *raises camera. A GREAT FLASH OF WHITE LIGHT. QUICK, JANGLED MUSIC.*)

GIRL. (*With a cry.*)
  Don't look! Cover your face!

(*The effect finished,* GIRL *breaks quickly to* D. R. *ramp.* SECOND REPORTER *races after her to position in "well" between* U. R. *wall of ring and upper ramp.* FIRST REPORTER, *simultaneously, darts out upper entrance of ring and stands at* L. *of* SECOND REPORTER. *They face* U. S., *backs to audience.*)

SARAH. (*Weakly.*)
  Mary! Jonathan!

(MR. ZUSS *raises mask.*)

J.B.
                    You bastards!
  (*He races out to upper ramp, looking for* REPORTERS.)
  I'll beat your goddam brains out. . . . Where have
      you
  Gone? . . . Answer me. . . .
  (SARAH *looks up at* MR. ZUSS, *who has raised his mask.*)

                    Answer me. . . . Answer
                  me.

(MR. ZUSS *lowers mask, hangs it up.*)

SARAH.

Why did you follow *them?* It wasn't
They that did it. . . . It wasn't they.
(MR. ZUSS *crosses* D. *to platform.* SARAH *watches* MR.
ZUSS.)
What had they done to Him . . . those children . . .

J.B. (*Turning back.*)

Don't, Sarah. Don't. It doesn't
Help to think that.

SARAH.

Doesn't . . . help . . . ?
What can help them—now?

J.B.

It . . . happened . . .

SARAH.

Yes! And who let it happen?

MR. ZUSS.

SHALL WE
TAKE THE GOOD AND NOT THE EVIL?

J.B.

SHALL WE TAKE THE GOOD AND NOT THE
EVIL? We have to take the evil—
Evil with good.
(*Crosses* L. *to* SARAH. *She cringes away, exits* L.
NICKLES *crosses* R. *to* U. C. *entrance.*)
It doesn't mean there
Is no good.

MR. ZUSS.

You *know* that. Don't you!

J.B.

Sticks and stones and steel are chances.
There's no will in stone and steel. . . .
It *happens* to us. . . .
(*Exit* L., *after* SARAH.)

SARAH. (*Off.*)

No! Don't touch me!

(GIRL *exits* D. R.)

NICKLES.
Starting, isn't it?

(NICKLES *runs* R. *on upper ramp, gets police raincoats from platform. Brings them along ramp, and hands one to each of the* REPORTERS, *who drop their hats to the floor.*)

MR. ZUSS.
Wait a minute.

(NICKLES *enters ring, as* REPORTERS *cross* R. *on upper ramp, getting into coats.*)

NICKLES.
Worried?

(REPORTERS *exit* D. R.)

MR. ZUSS.
No! Where are you going?

(NICKLES *crosses to* L. *of table.*)

NICKLES.
Just a walk in the earth for my health—or
Somebody's.
MR. ZUSS.
Leave him alone a minute.
NICKLES.
Who? Me? Am I . . . God?
(*Sets* D. S. *stool to* L. *of table, crosses* U. R. C.)
Why should we leave him alone? He's suffering.
It's an old role . . . played like a mouth organ.
Any fool on earth can learn. . . .
Despair in six, short, easy lessons!
Give him another little, needling
Nudge between the withers and the works:
He'll learn. . . . He's desperate now. . . . You'll
teach him.

(*Crosses through well* U. R. *to foot of platform steps* D. R.
Whistles. 1. SIREN, off R. *2. CAR DOOR SLAMS, off*

R. *3. MUSIC UNDER DIALOGUE. FIRST and SEC-*
OND POLICE OFFICERS hurry up ramp from D. R. J.B., a
coat thrown over his shoulders, runs up steps from U. L.,
to meet them and bring them into the ring, through U. C.
entrance. SECOND POLICE OFFICER has parasol, wrapped
in brown wrapping paper, hidden under his coat. He
places his hat on U. R. ring wall near U. C. entrance.
Stands, facing U. S. FIRST POLICE OFFICER enters to R.
of table. J.B. follows, to L. of table.)

FIRST POLICE OFFICER. (*Entering ring.*)
  Sorry to question you like this. We got to
  Get the story.
J.B. (*Crosses to L. entrance, calls off.*)
          Sarah! Sarah!

(SARAH *enters. FIRST POLICE OFFICER removes hat, gets*
out pencil and notebook, crosses L., puts hat on table,
and crosses around below table, sitting at L. of table.
SARAH enters from L., passes below J.B. She wears a
negligee. Sits above table. J.B. stands above her. NICKLES
crouches R. MR. ZUSS is on perch. MUSIC DIMS.)

FIRST POLICE OFFICER.
  Turning your house into a . . .
J.B.
                              It doesn't

  Matter.

(*MUSIC PLAYS TO ITS CONCLUSION UNDER*
DIALOGUE.)

SARAH.
          Nothing matters but to
  Know.
FIRST POLICE OFFICER.
          How many children?
J.B.
                              Two.

FIRST POLICE OFFICER.
  Girls?

SARAH.
          Our boys are . . . dead.
FIRST POLICE OFFICER.
                                        Girls.
  Names?
J.B.
          Ruth, Rebecca.
SARAH.
                                   Ruth is the
  Oldest.
FIRST POLICE OFFICER.
          And you saw her last?
J.B.
  Ruth?
SARAH.
     It's *Rebecca* is missing!
J.B.
                                        He
  Knows.
SARAH.
     No! It's God that knows! . . .

  (*Awkward silence.*)
  She's the littlest one. She's gone.
FIRST POLICE OFFICER.
  How long ago?
SARAH.
                         Oh . . . hours.
FIRST POLICE OFFICER.
  It's three in the morning now.
J.B.
                                   Since seven.

FIRST POLICE OFFICER.
  And you reported it . . . ?
J.B.
                              Yes.
FIRST POLICE OFFICER.
                                        When?

J.B.

One o'clock. A quarter after.
We looked for her everywhere, of course.
Then we thought—I thought—if somebody . . .
Maybe the telephone would ring.

FIRST POLICE OFFICER.

And you'd do better on your own!

J.B.

Yes.

SARAH.

Yes! Yes! Yes!
We believe in our luck in this house!
We've earned the right to! We believe in it . . .
All but the bad!

NICKLES. (*Leaning in to* D. R. *entrance of ring.*)
                That's telling him!

That's telling him!
    If God is Will
    And Will is well
    Then what is ill?
    God still?
    (*Front.*)
    Dew tell!

FIRST POLICE OFFICER.
                And nobody telephoned?

J.B.

Nobody telephoned.

FIRST POLICE OFFICER.
                            Dressed? How was she

Dressed?

J.B.
                White?

SARAH.

                White! *You* saw her—
    Glimmering in the twilight.

FIRST POLICE OFFICER.
                            White.

SARAH.

                            All but her

Shoes.

FIRST POLICE OFFICER.
          Her shoes were what?

SARAH.
                              Red.

FIRST POLICE OFFICER.
Rebecca have a red umbrella?

(MR. ZUSS *crosses to perch.* NICKLES *sees him go, unhooks mask and stick.*)

SARAH.
Parasol.

FIRST POLICE OFFICER.
          Little toy umbrella.

(J.B. *crosses* U. R. *of* SARAH.)

SARAH.
Parasol. Yes, she might have had one.

FIRST POLICE OFFICER.
You mean she owned one?

SARAH.
                    Yes. It belonged to a
Big doll we bought her once.
Scarlet silk. It opens and closes.
She kept it when the doll gave out.
She used to take it to bed with her even—
Open and close it.

J.B. (*Crosses to* U. L. SARAH.)
                    You've found the parasol!

(MR. ZUSS *raises mask, brings down drumstick. Lowers mask. DRUM BEAT SOUNDS off* R. *MUSIC UNDER.* SECOND POLICE OFFICER *turns front, the wrapped parcel in his hand.* SARAH *sees him, rises, crosses to* U. R. *of* J. B. FIRST POLICE OFFICER *rises, crosses to* L. *entrance, faces off* L. MR. ZUSS *holds mask and stick in down position.*)

SECOND POLICE OFFICER.
   What will it tell you? Will it tell you why?
   Out in the desert in the tombs
   Are potter's figures:
   (*Takes out pocket-knife. Opens it. Crosses to above
   table.*)
                         Two of warriors,
   Two of worthies, two of monsters.
   Ask them why. They will not answer you. . . .
   (*Cuts string.*)
   Can the tooth among the stones make answer? . . .
   (*Cuts string.*)
   Can the seven bones reply? . . .
   (*Cuts string.*)
   Death is a bone that stammers . . . a tooth
   (*Puts knife on table.*)
   Among the flints that has forgotten.

(*He unrolls parcel. Parasol drops onto table. He turns,
crosses* U. S., *picks up hat, puts it on; crosses onto upper
ramp, crumples paper, throws it off* U. R. J.B. *picks up
parasol, holds it close to his chest. He crosses below table
to* D. R. C.)

FIRST POLICE OFFICER.
   Just past midnight—quarter past—
   Pounding his beat by the back of the lumberyard
   Somebody runs and he yells and they stumble—
   Big kid—nineteen maybe—
   Hopped to the eyes and scared—scared
   Bloodless he could barely breathe.
   Constable yanks him up by the britches.
   (*Crosses to table to get pad and pencil and hat.*)
   "All right! Take me to it!"
   Just a shot in the dark, he was so
   Goddam scared there had to be something. . . .
   (*Crosses* D. R. *of table.*)
   Well . . . he took him to it. . . . Back of the

Lumber trucks beside the track.
It was tight in her fist when he found her—still.

(*Crosses out* U. C. *entrance, stands on upper ramp beside*
SECOND POLICE OFFICER.)

NICKLES. (*Leaning toward J.B.*)
Now's the time to say it, Mister.
MR. ZUSS.
Now *is* the time. . . . Now is the time. . . .
J.B.
THE LORD GIVETH. . . . THE LORD TAKETH
AWAY. . . . (*Sobs.*)

(SARAH *exits* L.)

MR. ZUSS.
Finish it! BLESSED BE THE . . .

(J.B. *starts* L.)

NICKLES.
What should he
Finish when he's said it all?
MR. ZUSS.
Go on!
NICKLES.
To what? To where? He's got there, hasn't he?
Now he's said it, now he knows.
He knows Who gives. He knows Who takes. . . .
MR. ZUSS.
Knows and accepts it all. All of it.

(J.B. *continues to* L. *entrance, holding parasol to his
chest.* OFFICERS *stand in well,* U. R. *of ring.*)

NICKLES. (*Crosses* C.)
Accepts it all! Accepts! A son
Destroyed by some fool officer's stupidity!
Two children smeared across a road
At midnight by a drunken child!
A daughter raped and murdered by **an idiot!**

And all with God's consent! Foreknowledge!
He *accepts* it!
(*Touches the knife on the table.*)

MR. ZUSS.
              He accepts it
All. And more! And blesses God!

NICKLES. (*Picks up knife, whirls to address* MR. ZUSS.)
You wait! He'll curse God to his face!

(MR. ZUSS *brings down drumstick, hangs up mask and
stick. MUSIC STARTS. LIGHTS CHANGE. SOUND.*
NICKLES *darts out* U. C., *down steps, and slashes at imaginary tent guy ropes with knife. Tent wall collapses.
In the ring, a section of the sidewall,* U. R. C., *breaks up-
ward crazily; and the sections* D. R. *and* D. L. *fall backward.* NICKLES *rushes* D. C., *shoves table off to* PROP MAN
in L. *entrance. Picks up two stools, whirls at* C., *tosses
first one stool, then the other off to* PROP MAN *in* L. *entrance. Darts* U. C., *then back to above trap door at*
U. C., *kicks at floor. Trap door opens, and glow of RED
LIGHT shoots up. Banners,* L., *fall to floor.* NICKLES
crosses U. C. *on ramp to* R. *of ring entrance. A procession
of* WOMEN *enters slowly from* U. L. *and up steps into
ring. They cough in the murk. First comes* MRS. ADAMS,
then MRS. MURPHY, *then* MRS. BOTTICELLI, MISS
MABEL, MRS. LESURE, JOLLY ⌊*carrying a small* BOY *on
her back*⌋. *The procession winds down the* L. *side of the
ring and across through* C. *below the trap door.*
NICKLES *moves to above trap.* MISS MABEL *bumps into*
BOTTICELLI *from behind.*)

BOTTICELLI.
Cripes! Look out with your feet, can't you?

(ADAMS *continues to* D. R. *ramp, followed to* R. *edge of
ring by* MURPHY.)

MISS MABEL.
How can a lady look out with her feet?
It's hard enough with your eyes in this smother.
(*Crosses* U. S. *to* R. *of trap.*)

Boy.
  I'm cold.

(BOTTICELLI *crosses* U. R.)

LESURE. (*Crosses* D. C.)
        Catch a hold of my skirt.
JOLLY.
  He's cold: wet and cold.
BOY.
                        I'm *cold.*
MURPHY. (D. R. *edge of ring.*)
  Somebody give me a finger to follow:
  There isn't a walk or a wall . . .

(BOTTICELLI *has crossed onto* D. R. *ramp near ring.* MISS
MABEL *hurries forward to help* MURPHY, *crossing* D. R.
in ring.)

BOTTICELLI.
                        You'll fall.

(MISS MABEL *crosses* D., *helps* MURPHY.)

ADAMS. (R. *on* D. R. *ramp.*)
  Even the Liggetts is gone.

(MISS MABEL *crosses* D. *on* R. *ramp.*)

BOY.
                        Mother! I'm
  Cold!
LESURE.
        I know. I know.
ADAMS. (*Turns* L., *almost bumps into* MISS MABEL.)
                        Land's
  Sakes! Oh . . . it's *you!*
BOTTICELLI. (*Picks up footstool,* R. *of ring.*)
                        Who?
ADAMS. (*To* MISS MABEL.)
  Where are you headed?

MISS MABEL. (*Crosses* D. R.)
> Wherever I'm going.

LESURE.
> Where has she ever, but to bed?

(ADAMS *crawls down lower ramp to a position below the ring.*)

BOTTICELLI.
> There isn't a bed in the town: they've foundered.

MISS MABEL. (D. R.)
> You ought to know. You've been into enough of them.

MURPHY. (*Sitting on* D. R. *edge of stage level, above* D. S. *ramp.*)
> And that's the truth if the kettle does say it!

BOTTICELLI. (*Hovering over* MURPHY.)
> Call me a pot, I'll tear your hair!

LESURE. (*Clambering over edge of ring,* D. S. C.)
> Aiye!

BOTTICELLI. (*Putting stool down at* R. *of ring.*)
> What?

LESURE.
> It's like a wall.

ADAMS.
> At least it's the lee of the wind. That's something.

LESURE.
> Lie by the wall, child.

(JOLLY *hands* BOY *down to* LESURE, *clambers down after him.* BOY *snuggles down in* LESURE'S *lap,* JOLLY *at their* L.)

MURPHY. (*Carries a copy of "The News." Hands it to* LESURE.)
> Here's the papers.
> All we've got's the *News.* It's small.

MISS MABEL. (*Crosses* R., *sits below bow of stairs.*)
> The *Times* goes all over you.

(MR. ZUSS *and* NICK *exchange a look.*)

LESURE.
                      Don't they, though.

ADAMS.
   Don't what?
   (*Stuffs papers under overhanging edge of ring.*)
MURPHY.
              The times. They go over you.
   (*Settles on lower ramp.*)
BOTTICELLI. (*Sitting on stool, R. of ring.*)
                        Ahhhh!

(*A drowsy silence.*)

MURPHY.
   I fell asleep in the hall like I told you—
   Woke in the alley.
BOTTICELLI. (*Half asleep.*)
                Yes . . . you told.
LESURE.
   We slept in the parlor and woke on the roof.
JOLLY.
   Only there wasn't one.
BOTTICELLI. (*Yawn.*)
                Yes . . . we know. . . .
MISS MABEL. (*Lighting cigarette.*)
   Know what there was in the crib of the ark
   When the world went down? . . . Four old women.
LESURE.
   What's the good of four old women?
ADAMS.
   Go on sailing in the dark.
J.B. (*Off U. L.*)
                Sarah! . . .
   Sarah! . . . Sarah! . . . Ruth! . . . Sarah! . . .

(NICKLES *looks* U. L. *for* J.B. WOMEN *look toward the sound of the voice.*)

MURPHY.
   Somebody calling his girl in the middle of
   That!

BOTTICELLI.
    The blessing of blood's coming back in me.
I'm warm to the knees.

(SECOND CIVIL DEFENSE OFFICER *enters* D. R. *and goes up upper ramp toward* C., *carrying* SARAH. FIRST CIVIL DEFENSE OFFICER *follows, carrying lighted flashlight.*)

MURPHY.
                        Squeeze in.
ADAMS.
                        I'm squeezing.
MISS MABEL. (*Singing to herself.*)
    . . . who when we court and kiss
    She cries: O Sir, let go!
    But when we come where comfort is
    She never will say no.

(OFFICER *carries* SARAH *to* U. C. *entrance of ring.* J.B., *with a final, "Sarah" enters from* L. *to them.* NICKLES *moves above the group, permitting* FIRST OFFICER *to join others.* D. S., JOLLY *crawls to a position on ramp at* D. R. *of ring, near onstage tent peg, watches, crouching, her tattered covering wrapped around her shoulders.*)

FIRST CDO.
    She said she lived around here somewhere.
    This is all there is.
J.B. (*His clothes torn, dust-covered.*)
                        Sarah!
FIRST CDO.
    Where do you want her? On the floor?
    You're lucky, boy. You've got a floor.

(SECOND CDO *carries* SARAH, *who is in tattered, dusty attire, to a position* D. L. C. *in ring, puts her down; crouches at her* L. J.B. *kneels at her* R. FIRST CDO *moves* D. R. *in ring and to* R. *of them.*)

J.B.
    Where was she?

(NICKLES *is at* U. C. *entrance.*)

FIRST CDO.
                    Underneath a wall.
He heard her underneath a wall.
(*Indicates other* OFFICER.)
Tell him what you heard her . . .
SECOND CDO.
                                        I heard
Two words. I don't know what they mean.
(*Imitating a voice calling.*)
Ruth! . . . Ruth! . . .

(BOY *whimpers "Mama."* SECOND CDO *rises, unfastens his canteen, takes it across, above, to* D. C., *hands it to* LESURE, *who gives* BOY *a drink, then she hands canteen back to* SECOND CDO, *who crouches at* D. S. *edge of ring.*)

FIRST CDO. (*At* R. *of* J.B.)
                    Nobody answered:
Nobody could have. You been down there?
Whole block's gone. Bank block. All of it.
J.B.'s bank, you know. Just gone
Nothing left to show it ever . . .
Just the hole. (*Crosses* R.)
                    J.B.'s millions!
That's a laugh now—J.B.'s millions!
All he's got is just the hole.
Plant went, too—all of it—everything.
(*Indicates* SECOND CDO.)
Ask him! Just the hole. He'll tell you.
SARAH. (*Stirring.*)
Ruth! . . . Ruth! . . .
FIRST CDO.
                    He can tell you.
He can tell you what he saw.

(SECOND CDO *crosses to* U. R. *of* J.B.)

SARAH.
David . . . Jonathan . . . Mary . . . Ruth . . .
I cannot say the last.

J.B.
                                        Rebecca.

SARAH.
David . . . Jonathan . . . Mary . . . Ruth . . .

J.B. (*To* SECOND CDO.)
You didn't find . . . ? There wasn't . . . ?

SECOND CDO.
                                                    I heard
Two words. I don't know what they mean.
I have brought them to you like a pair of pebbles.
Picked up in a path or a pair of
Beads that might belong to somebody.

J.B.
There wasn't . . . anyone besides . . . ?

(*DISTANT SIREN.* OFFICERS *and* WOMEN *look off* R.)

SECOND CDO.
I ONLY AM ESCAPED ALONE TO TELL THEE.

(*LOUD SIREN, off* R. *MUSIC.* OFFICERS *slowly exit,*
D. R. WOMEN *fall asleep.*)

SARAH.
David . . . Jonathan . . . (*She sobs.*)

NICKLES.
                                        It isn't decent!
It isn't moral even. It's disgusting!
(*Crosses to* U. L. *of* J.B.)
His weeping wife in her despair,
(*MUSIC FADES OUT.*)
And he beside her on his trembling **ham bones**
Taking it! *Eating* it! It isn't *decent!*

MR. ZUSS.
You don't lose gracefully, do you?

NICKLES.
                                        I don't
Lose.

MR. ZUSS.
    You have.

(*TRAP DOOR CLOSES.*)

DISTANT VOICE.
    HAST THOU CONSIDERED MY SERVANT JOB?
MR. ZUSS.
                    Put on your mask.
(*Puts up mask, unhooks stick.* NICKLES *crosses* D. L.,
puts mask up.)

GODMASK.
    HAST THOU CONSIDERED
        MY SERVANT JOB?
DISTANT VOICE.
    THAT THERE IS NONE LIKE
        HIM ON THE EARTH.
GODMASK.
    THAT THERE IS NONE LIKE   (*These speeches
        HIM ON THE EARTH.   tend to overlap;
DISTANT VOICE.   with* MR. ZUSS
    AND STILL HE HOLDETH   *picking up his
        FAST HIS INTEGRITY.   cues from* DIS-
GODMASK.   TANT VOICE.*)
    AND STILL HE HOLDETH
        FAST HIS INTEGRITY.

(NICKLES *crosses* D. L., *puts on
mask.*)

DISTANT VOICE.
ALTHOUGH THOU MOVEDST
    ME AGAINST HIM.
GODMASK.
ALTHOUGH THOU MOVEDST
    ME AGAINST HIM.

DISTANT VOICE.
    TO DESTROY HIM . . .
GODMASK.
                        TO DESTROY HIM . . .

DISTANT VOICE.

> WITHOUT CAUSE,

GODMASK.

> WITHOUT CAUSE.

(SARAH *rises, crosses above* J.B.)

SATANMASK.
  SKIN FOR SKIN, YEA, ALL THAT A MAN
  HATH WILL HE GIVE FOR HIS LIFE
  BUT PUT FORTH THINE HAND NOW . . .
    AND TOUCH HIS
  BONE AND HIS FLESH . . . AND HE WILL
  CURSE THEE TO THY FACE!
GODMASK.

> BEHOLD

  HE IS IN THINE HAND BUT
    (MR. ZUSS *brings down drumstick.*)

> SAVE HIS LIFE.

(*DRUMBEAT.* MR. ZUSS *lowers mask, hangs up mask
and stick. RED LIGHT springs up in ring area.* SARAH
stares at J.B.*'s back. She gasps as* J.B. *stiffens in pain.*
MISS MABEL *crosses to* D. R. *ring entrance, watching.*
JOLLY *rises to knees, watching.* WOMEN *watch.*)

J.B.
  God, let me die! God, let me die!

(MR. ZUSS *starts down.* SARAH *touches* J.B.*'s back. He
winces in pain.*)

NICKLES.
  I don't lose.
MR. ZUSS.

> You have. (*Crosses to platform.*)

NICKLES. (*Crosses* U. S. *at* L.)

> There's still the

  Pain. God asks the proof of pain,
  Of physical agony, the last, the worst,

The furthest suffering the nerves can bear:
He needs the proof of pain from each of us:
Hunts us through our branching veins
With agony . . . until we . . . *give it.*
MR. ZUSS.
    Job will support the proof of pain.
NICKLES. (*Crosses to* U. R. *of* J.B.)
    Not even Job. Not now. Not after
    That! Look at him! Look at him!
MR. ZUSS.

                                    Even if
    God must seal him in his sack of skin
    And scald his skin to crust to squeeze
    The answer out, he'll answer.
NICKLES.

                                    No!
    Job will make his own cold peace.
    A man can always cease. It's something—
    A judgment anyway—reject
    The whole creation with a stale pink pill.
ADAMS.
    Poor soul!
BOTICELLI.
                Look at them *burns* on him!
LESURE. (*To* BOY.)
    Don't look, child. You'll remember them.
JOLLY.
    Every sore I seen I remember.
BOTTICELLI.
    Look at them burns! Look at them *burns!*
MISS MABEL.
    His skin looks like . . .
BOTICELLI.

                        Don't!
MISS MABEL.

                                . . . They'd *flayed* it!
    Tatters of torn shirt . . . it looks like.
LESURE.
    Poor soul! Poor soul!

BOTTICELLI.
　That's his wife.
MISS MABEL.
　　　　　　　Whose wife? Whose?
MURPHY.
　You know. You've seen her picture.
J.B.
　　　　　　　　　　　　　God, let me
　Die!
SARAH.
　　　　　You think He'd *let* you? God is our
　Enemy.
J.B.
　　　　Don't say that, Sarah. God
　Has something hidden from our hearts to show.
MISS MABEL.
　She knows. She's looking at it.
J.B.
　　　　　　　　　　　　Try to
　Sleep.

(SARAH *lies* U. R. *of* J.B., *her head toward* D. R.)

MISS MABEL.
　　　　　He should have kept it hidden.
　(*Crosses* D. R. *on ramp.*)
J.B.
　Once I knew a charm for sleep—

　　Not as forgetfulness but gift,
　　Not as sleep but second sight,
　　Come and from my eyelids lift
　　The dead of night.
SARAH.
　　　　　　　The dead of night.
　Come and from my eyelids lift
　The dead . . . of night. . . .
J.B.
　　　　　　　　　　Out of sleep

Something of our own comes back to us . . .
A drowned man's garment from the sea.
ADAMS.
All that's left him now is her.
LESURE.
Still that's something—a good woman.
MURPHY.
What good is a woman to him with that hide on
    him ——?
Or he to her—if you think of it?
LESURE.

Don't then.

MISS MABEL. (*Crosses to* R. *of* MURPHY.)
Can you blame her?
MURPHY.

I don't blame her.

All I say is, she's no comfort.
She won't cuddle.
LESURE. (*To* MURPHY.)

What's got into you?

MISS MABEL. (*Settling beside* MURPHY.)
Nothing recently, I'll hazard.
LESURE.
None of that! We have a child here. . . .
MURPHY. (*To* MISS MABEL.)
Roll a little nearer, dearie,
Me backside's froze. . . .

(MISS MABEL *cuddles closer*.)

You smell of roses.

MISS MABEL.
Neither do you, but you're warm.
BOTTICELLI.

Well—

Good-night, ladies.
(*She starts song, and* MURPHY, LESURE *and* ADAMS
join in.)

Good-night, ladies . . .

(MISS MABEL *joins song on third line*. NICKLES *crosses*
L. *to* U. S. *entrance*.)

SARAH. (*Screams at end of third line of song, jerking
herself up.*)
 Oh, my babies! My poor babies!

(*The* WOMEN *cut short their song.*)

J.B. (*Gently.*)
 Go back to sleep.
SARAH. (*Kneeling at* R. *of* J.B.)
     Go! Go where?
 If there were darkness I'd go there.
 If there were night I'd lay me down in it.
 God has shut the night against me.
 God has set the dark alight
 With horror blazing blind as day
 When I go toward it . . . close my eyes.
J.B.
 I know . . . I know those waking eyes.
 (*He is silent a moment.*)
 His will is everywhere against me.
 Even in my sleep . . . my dreams.
 (*Pause.*)
 If I knew! If I knew *why!*
 What I can't bear is . . . the blindness . . .
 Meaninglessness . . . the numb blow
 Fallen in the stumbling night.
SARAH.
 Even *this*—has it no meaning?
J.B.
 God will not punish without cause.
 God is God or we are nothing—
 Mayflies that leave their husks behind—
 Our tiny lives ridiculous—a suffering
 Not even sad that Someone Somewhere
 Laughs at, as we laugh at apes.
 God is unthinkable if we are innocent.
SARAH.
 Oh, my dear, my dear, my dear,

Does God demand deception of us—
Purchase His innocence with ours?
Must we be guilty *for* Him?—bear
The burden of the world's malevolence
For Him who made the world?

J.B.

                              God is

Just!

SARAH.

     God is just!
(*Rise, crosses above to* L. *of* J.B.)
                    If God is
Just, our slaughtered, broken children
Stank with sin . . . were rotten with it!

J.B. (*Takes her hand, she kneels.*)

                              Sarah!

Even desperate we can't despair. . . .
(NICKLES *moves to* L. *entrance.* SARAH *tries to pull her
hand from* J.B.)
No! Don't let my hand go, Sarah.
Say it after me: THE LORD
GIVETH . . . Say it!

SARAH.

                    THE LORD GIVETH . . .

J.B.

THE LORD TAKETH AWAY. . . .

SARAH. (*Rising.*)

                              Takes!

Kills! Kills! Kills! Kills!

J.B.

BLESSED BE THE NAME OF THE LORD.

SARAH.

                              They are

Dead! And they were innocent! I will not
Let you sacrifice their deaths
To make injustice justice and God good!
Must we buy quiet with their innocence—
Theirs and yours?

(*Crosses* L.)

　　　　　　　I cannot stay here—
I cannot stay here if you cringe
Connive in death's injustice, kneel to it—
Not if you betray my children.

J.B.

I have no choice but to be guilty.

SARAH.

We have the choice to live or die
All of us. (*Screaming.*)

　　　　　　　Curse God and die!

(*She kneels beside J.B. J.B. looks at her, then away. She repeats the words gently.*)

Curse God . . . and die!

(*She looks to J.B. for answer. He looks at her, then away.*)

J.B.

BLESSED
BE THE NAME OF THE LORD. . . .

(*MUSIC. MR. ZUSS lifts his hands. SARAH rises, moves to* L. *entrance.* MR. ZUSS *lowers hands. She moves down* L. *steps, into pit, past* WOMEN, *who draw back to let her pass. She crosses up* R. *side, and as she passes* JOLLY *at top of ramp,* JOLLY *spits at* SARAH. SARAH *staggers out* D. R. *FADE MUSIC OUT.*)

MURPHY.

　　　　　　　　　　What did I
Say? Eh? His hide was too much for her.

BOTTICELLI.

His hide or his heart.

MURPHY.

　　　　　　　The hide comes between.

LESURE.

The heart is the stranger.

BOTTICELLI.

> Oh! Strange!
It's always strange the heart is.

(*RUSHING WIND.*)

MISS MABEL.

> Only
It's the skin we ever know.

J.B. (*Reaching out for the vanished* SARAH, *moves around to his* L. *in complete, helpless circle on his knees.*)
Sarah! . . . Sarah! . . . Why do you not speak to
me?
Sarah! . . .

MISS MABEL.

> Now he knows.

MURPHY.

> And he's alone now.

(WOMEN *hum.* BOTTICELLI *gets up, moves into the ring to* R. *of* J.B.)

BOTTICELLI.
You're cold. Cold. Come down with the rest of us.
Come down with the rest. We'll keep you warm.
There's four or five of us out of the wind there
Keeping each other warm. Come down.

J.B.
SHOW ME MY GUILT, O GOD!

(*Falls forward.* BOTTICELLI *returns to the stool above ramp outside ring,* R., *as* JOLLY *crosses into ring to* L. *of* J.B., *removes her shawl, spreads it carefully over* J.B.'s *back, walking above him to his* R. *as she does so.* WOMEN *rise, start up ramp* R., *to form a line to enter the ring.*)

NICKLES.
Well? You going to show him?

MR. ZUSS.

> Wait!

Wait!

(BOY *moves to stand in front of* MISS MABEL *above ramp, at* R. *entrance of ring.* WOMEN *enter ring, and stand below* J.B. *in a half-circle. They kneel before him, humming.* JOLLY *kneels in her place by his side.* MISS MABEL *and* BOY *remain* D. R., *watching.*)

J.B. (*Rising, to knees, arms out.*)
    SHOW ME MY GUILT, O GOD!

(WOMEN *reach up to pull him down. LIGHTS fade out. Gauze CURTAIN drops in front of ring. HOUSE LIGHTS. When the house lights are up,* MR. ZUSS *crosses down from platform, through ring, and out at* L. *Group* C. *The* WOMEN *rise and await his exit. When they rise,* J.B. *and* NICKLES *exit* L. WOMEN, BOTTICELLI, GIRL *and* BOY *follow out at* L. *in formal procession.*)

THE FIRST ACT IS OVER

INTERMISSION

ACT TWO

*At end of Act One tent-wall at back has been lowered
to floor. Flame drop has been exchanged for sky
drop at rear. House lights are on, and gauze curtain
is still in place in front of ring area.*

SECOND ROUSTABOUT (*as per identification in Act One*)
enters, L., *unhooks* D. S. *clip on recumbent banner-
canopy, which still lies on ramp* L. *Then he crosses
into ring, re-sets displaced* L. *wall of ring; moves*
U. C., *re-sets displaced* U. S. *ring wall section; crosses*
R., *replaces* R. *displaced ring wall section. As he
crosses* C., FIRST ROUSTABOUT *enters,* L., *carrying an
armful of nondescript rags, which he piles in the*
C. *of ring area. At* D. R., SECOND ROUSTABOUT *sig-
nals.* FIRST ROUSTABOUT *to follow him, they exit*
D. R. *HOUSE LIGHTS DIM TO HALF. Actors
enter via* L. *ramp and assume their places (with ex-
ception of the* BOY, *who does not re-appear.). Order
of entrance:* MR. ZUSS, BOTTICELLI, MISS MABEL,
MURPHY, ADAMS, LESURE, JOLLY, NICKLES. *Under
cover of their crossing to positions,* J.B., *wrapped in
the covering* JOLLY *placed over him at the end of Act
One, crawls to his place at* C. *of ring area, cowering
on his knees, his head buried in his hands; the pile
of rags beneath him.* WOMEN, *except* JOLLY, *are
asleep. When actors are in position, MUSIC.
HOUSE LIGHTS DIM OUT. Gauze curtain flies
out in dark. STAGE LIGHTS come up.* J.B. *strug-
gles, moaning slightly.*

JOLLY. (*Noticing* J.B.)
   Mother!

(WOMEN *awaken.*)

81

LESURE.
         Scrabbling up with that *crust* on him!
MURPHY.
     How can he struggle in that . . . crust of *pain?*
MISS MABEL.
     He has to struggle. He can't just lie there.
     He's a human being, isn't he?
BOTTICELLI.
     Know what humanity is? A potato!
     Tramp it deep enough it . . . grows.
MISS MABEL.
     Even old and dry, it flourishes.
MURPHY.
     Don't I know! Don't I know!
J.B. (*Has risen to knees, looks up.*)
     SHOW ME MY GUILT, O GOD!
MR. ZUSS. (*On platform.*)
     Nickles. The time has come, Nickles—
     Remember those proud prophecies of yours?
     Take everything he had and he'd curse God?
     Touch him in the flesh and he'd curse God?
     Well, have you heard him cursing God?
     (WOMEN *doze.*)
     God has done everything you asked for:
     God has destroyed him without cause. . . .
NICKLES. (*Crosses to above J.B.*)
     God has destroyed his *wealth,* his *children,*
     Stripped raw tatters from his *skin,*
     Touched his *flesh,* but him himself
     God has not touched. Teach his soul!
     (*Crosses* R. *toward* WOMEN.)
     Show him that there are no reasons!
     Show him neither God nor man
     Has reasons adequate to his catastrophes!
     Do you think he'll call God then?
     Not in that voice, anyway!
MR. ZUSS.
     Touch him where you please. You've lost him.

J.B.
  SHOW ME MY GUILT, O GOD!
NICKLES. (*Crosses* D. S.)

                        Silence!
  The still silence of the stars! (*Looks at* J.B.)
J.B. (*Crawling* D. C.)
  Is there not anyone to answer me?
  Where is the wisdom of this world
  That once knew answers where there were no answers?
  Where are the answerers to answer it?
NICKLES. (*Crosses* U. C., *speaks to* MR. ZUSS.)
                        Silence!
  The slow silence of the soul!
J.B. (*To the audience, crawling a little forward, a whisper.*)
  The hand of God has touched me. Look at me!
  Every hope I ever had,
  Every task I put my will to,
  Every work I've ever done,
  Annulled as though I had not done it.
  My trace extinguished in the land.
  (NICKLES *crosses to above* J.B.)
  My children dead. My father's name
  Obliterated in the sunlight. . . . Answer me!
  Answer me! Answer me! Answer me! Answer me!

(*Hides head. Darkness. Silence. Sound of DRUM-BEATS. On the upper ramp,* ELIPHAZ *enters from* L.; ZOPHAR *over* C. *from behind ramp;* BILDAD *climbs up over* R. *end ramp. They move to* C. *entrance* U. S.; ELIPHAZ *dressed in office attire* [*tattered and dusty*] *of a psychiatrist, with a ragged coat draped over his shoulders.* ZOPHAR *in the rumpled garb of a cleric; his collar missing;* BILDAD *in an ancient leather jacket, the uniform of the professional proletarian.* ELIPHAZ *holds a cigarette in a damaged, elegant holder;* ZOPHAR *carries a cigar;* BILDAD *has a pipe.* NICKLES' *back is to the trio, but he senses their presence. MUSIC continues under dialogue.*)

NICKLES.
  Mr. Zuss! Who *are* they?

  (*Turns to face the* TRIO.)
MR. ZUSS.
                            Comforters.
NICKLES.
  What comforters?
MR. ZUSS.
                            Job's Comforters.
  Every time they play this play
  Job's Comforters must come . . . to comfort him.
NICKLES. (*Backing* D. S.)
  You mean to justify the ways of God to
  God by making *Job* responsible.
  Making him . . . worthy of his . . . wretchedness.
  (*Crosses* R. *below* J.B.)
  Giving him that dear gift of guilt,
  That putrid poultice of the soul that sucks
  The poison in not out! That dirty
  Thumb our generation relishes.
  (*Crosses* R. *to beneath platform.*)
MR. ZUSS.
  What are you afraid of, Nickles?
  Afraid he'll find the fault his own—
  His folly—and be comforted?

(*The* COMFORTERS, *peering in the* U. C. *entrance, are
smiling knowingly. On* MR. ZUSS' *word: "folly" in the
above speech, each lights a match and applies it to his
smoke.* JOLLY *is startled by the match flame.*)

JOLLY.
  Look! Look! Look! Look!
  Mother! Mother!

(*The* WOMEN *notice the* COMFORTERS.)

MURPHY.
                            Christ! Those eyes!

MISS MABEL.
Look at them! They hate each other!
Each one knows the truth . . . alone.

(*The* COMFORTERS *move:* BILDAD *to* R. *around the ring,
and eventually across the lower ramp to his position between the other two at the* L. *ring entrance;* ZOPHAR
along L. *of ring to steps* D. S. L.; ELIPHAZ, *by same route
to* L. *entrance.*)

LESURE.
That doctor one! He makes me creep.
ADAMS.
Creep! What brings him here, I wonder?
MISS MABEL.
The human smell of heart-sick misery.
LESURE.
Who's the collar?
MURPHY.
                    Some great preacher.

(ZOPHAR *blesses audience; crosses back* U. S. *to position
at* L. *entrance.*)

BOTTICELLI. (*Watching* BILDAD.)
See that leather-backed old bucket?
Call you Comrade in the park—
Blow your brains out in the cellar!
MURPHY. (*Indicating* ZOPHAR.)
Same with him. He'll damn your soul to
Hell for saying prayers he don't say.

(*As* BILDAD *joins the other* COMFORTERS *at* L. *entrance,
THE SOUND OF MUSIC FADES AWAY. The* COM-
FORTERS *peer into the ring, smiling sympathetically at*
J.B.)

J.B.
Thank God! You have come! You have come!
(*Silence.*)
I know how ludicrous I must look,

Covered with rags, my skin pustulent . . .
(*Silence.*)
I know . . . I know how others see me.
(*Silence.*)
Come in! Come in! I have no chairs now. . . .
(COMFORTERS *enter ring.* ZOPHAR *sits* D. L. C.; BILDAD
sits at J.B.'S L.; *when they are seated,* ELIPHAZ *sits
between them.*)
Speak to me! *Speak* to me! I sit here
Such as you see me. In my soul
I suffer what you guess I suffer.
Tell me the wickedness that justifies it?
What have I *done? What* . . . *have* . . . *I* . . . *done?*
BILDAD. (*Knocking out his pipe.*)
Fair question, Big Boy.
ZOPHAR. (*Crushing out his cigar.*)
                         Nonsense!
That was answered long ago—
Long ago.
ELIPHAZ. (*Removes glasses.*)
             In dreams are answers.
How do your dreams go, J.B.? Tell!
J.B. (*Staring in bewilderment from face to face.*)
I called into the night for answers.
BILDAD.
And we heard you.
ZOPHAR.
                 And we came.
J.B.
I called God.
BILDAD.
              And God was silent.
ZOPHAR.
God will not Himself reply
From the blue depths of His Eternity.
ELIPHAZ.
Blind depths of His Unconsciousness.
BILDAD.
Blank depths of His Necessity.

ZOPHAR.

God is far above in Mystery.

ELIPHAZ.

God is far within in Mindlessness.

BILDAD.

God is far beyond in History.

How can God have time for you?

J.B.

I have no children any more. . . .

Love too has left me.

BILDAD.

                Love!

What's love to Him? One man's misery!

J.B.

If I am innocent?

BILDAD.

                Innocent? Innocent?

Nations have perished in their innocence.

Classes have perished in their innocence.

Young men in slaughtered cities

Offering their silly throats

Against the tanks in innocence have perished.

What's your innocence to theirs?

God is History. If you offend Him

Will not History dispense with you?

History has no time for innocence.

J.B.

God is just. We are not squeezed

Naked through a ridiculous orifice

Like bulls into a blazing ring

To blunder here by blindfold laws

We never learn or can, deceived by

Stratagems and fooled by feints,

For sport, for nothing, till we fall

We're pricked so badly. God is just.

God is just.

BILDAD.

                Screw your justice!

History is justice!—time

Inexorably turned to truth!—
Not for one man. For humanity.
(*Rises, points to* J.B.)
One man s life won't measure on it.
One man's suffering won't count, no matter
What his suffering. But All *will*.
(*Crosses* D. R. *to proscenium.*)
At the end there will be justice!—
Justice for All! Justice for everyone!
On the way . . . it doesn't matter.
(*Crosses* D. R.)

MR. ZUSS. (*To* NICKLES.)
He calls that comfort?

NICKLES.

                Millions do.

J.B. (*Crawls* R., *looks after* BILDAD. ELIPHAZ *pockets glasses.*)
Guilt matters. Guilt must always matter.
Unless guilt matters the whole world is
Meaningless. God too is nothing.

BILDAD. (*A step toward* J.B.)
Guilt is a sociological accident.
Wrong class: wrong century.
You pay for your luck with your licks, that's all.
(*Crosses* R., *leans against stair rail.*)

ELIPHAZ.
Come! Come! Come! Guilt is a
Psychophenomenal situation—
An illusion, a disease, a sickness:
(J.B. *crawls to him.*)
That filthy feeling at the fingers,
Scent of dung beneath the nails. . . .

ZOPHAR.
Guilt is illusion? Guilt is reality!
The one reality there is!
All mankind are guilty always!

BILDAD.
The Fall of Man! It felled us all!

MR. ZUSS. (*To* NICKLES.)
They don't sound much like Comforters to me.
NICKLES.
Every generation has its own.
J.B. (*To* ELIPHAZ.)
Guilt matters. Guilt must always matter.

(BILDAD *crosses* R., *turns back.*)

ELIPHAZ.
No. We have surmounted guilt. It's quite
Quite different, isn't it? You see the difference.
Science knows now that the sentient spirit
Floats like the chambered nautilus on a sea
That drifts it under skies that drive:
Beneath, the sea of the subconscious;
Above, the winds that wind the world.
Caught between that sky, that sea,
Self has no will, cannot be guilty.
The sea drifts. The sky drives.
The tiny, shining bladder of the soul
Washes with wind and wave or shudders
Shattered between them.
ZOPHAR.
                              Blasphemy!
    (*Rise, crosses* U. L.)
BILDAD.
                                        Bullshit!

(NICKLES, *crossing* D. L., *reacts to this with a knowing
smile.*)

ELIPHAZ.
There is no guilt, my friend. We all are
Victims of our guilt—not guilty.
Our will is underneath the sybil's
Stone—not known.
J.B. (*Pause.*)
                    I'd rather suffer
Every unspeakable suffering God sends,
Knowing it was I that suffered,

I that earned the need to suffer,
I that acted, I that chose,
Than wash my hands with yours in that
Defiling innocence. Can we be men
And make an irresponsible ignorance
Responsible for everything?
I will not listen to you!
(*Ducks his head, pulls rags over it.*)

ELIPHAZ. (*Rising, crosses* U. S. C.)

But you will. . . .

MR. ZUSS.
There was a time when men found pity
Finding each other in the night:
Misery to walk with misery;
Brother in whose brother guilt
Guilt could be conceived and recognized.
(*Indicates trio.*)
Now comfort has forgotten pity.

ZOPHAR. (*Crosses to* L. *of* J.B.)
Ah, my son, how well you said that!
How well you said it! Without guilt
What is a man? An animal, isn't he?
A wolf forgiven at his meat,
(J.B. *raises head.*)
A beetle innocent in his copulation.
What divides us from the universe
Of blood and seed, conceives the soul in us,
Brings us to God, but guilt? The lion
Dies of death: we die of suffering.
The lion vanishes: our souls accept
Eternities of reparation.
But for our guilt we too would vanish,
Bundles of corrupting bones
Bagged in a hairless hide and rotting.
Happy the man whom God correcteth!
He tastes his guilt. His hope begins.
He is in league with the stones in certainty.

J.B. (*Crawls to* ZOPHAR.)
Teach me and I will hold my tongue.

Show me my transgression.
ZOPHAR. (*Kneels at* L. *of* J.B.)

               No,
No, my son. You show me.
Search your inmost heart! Question it!
Guilt is a deceptive secret,
The labor often of years, a work
Conceived in infancy, brought to birth
In unpredictable forms years after:
At twelve the palpable elder brother;
At seventeen, perhaps, the servant
Seen by the lamp by accident. . . .
J.B. (*Taking* ZOPHAR'S *hands.*)

               My
Sin! Teach me my sin! My wickedness!
(MR. ZUSS *and* NICKLES *react to* J.B.'s *violence.*)
Surely iniquity that suffers
Judgment like mine cannot be secret.
Mine is no childish fault, no nastiness
Concealed behind a bathroom door,
No sin a prurient virtue practices
Licking the silence from its lips
Like sugar afterwards. Mine is flagrant,
Worthy of death, of many deaths,
Of shame, loss, hurt—indignities
Such as *these!* Such as *these!*
Speak of the sin I must have sinned
To suffer what you see me suffer.
ZOPHAR.

Do we need to name our sins
To know the need to be forgiven?
Repent, my son! Repent!
J.B.

               Shall I
Repent of sins I have not sinned
To understand it? Till I die
I will not violate my integrity.

(COMFORTERS *shout with laughter.* BILDAD *moves* R. *to*

U. R. *of* J.B. ELIPHAZ *crosses to* D. L. *of* J.B. NICKLES
crosses U. S. *a step.* ZOPHAR *crosses to* U. S. *of* J.B.)
ZOPHAR.

>Your integrity! Your integrity!
>What integrity have you?
>A man, a miserable, mortal, sinful
>Venal man like any other!

BILDAD.

>A statistic! Like another!

ELIPHAZ.

>A case-history!

ZOPHAR.

>   Your integrity!
>You squat there challenging the universe
>To tell you what your sin is called,
>Thinking, because your life is virtuous,
>It can't be called. It can! Your sin is
>Simple! You were born a man!

BILDAD.

>   Your sin is
>Simple. You were born One Man.
>(*Crosses* U. S. *to upper ramp.*)

ELIPHAZ.

>Your sin *is* simple: you have none.
>You are a leaf the wind blows through.
>Flutter?—it's the wind, not you.
>(*Crosses* U. C., *to* L. *of* BILDAD.)

J.B. (*Pulls* ZOPHAR *around to him, clutching at his
trouser-leg.*)

>What is my *fault?* What have I done?

ZOPHAR.

>What is your fault? Man's heart is evil!
>What have you done? Man's will is evil!
>Your fault, your sin, are heart and will:
>The worm at heart, the wilful will
>Corrupted with its foul imagining.
>(*Crosses* D. L.)

J.B. (*Crawls after* ZOPHAR *forcing him* D. L. JOLLY

crawls a step after J.B. MURPHY, LESURE *and* ADAMS
rise to knees, watching.)

    Yours is the cruelest comfort of them all,
    Making the Creator of the Universe
    The miscreator of mankind—
    A party to the crimes He punishes . . .
    Making my sin a horror . . . a deformity!
ZOPHAR.
    If it were otherwise, we could not bear it.
J.B.
    I can bear anything a man can bear
    If I can *be* one—if my life
    Somehow can justify my living—
    If my own self can answer. You
    Refuse me even that. You tell me
    One man's guilt is meaningless—
    History has no time for guilt—
    Science has no sign for guilt—
    God created all men guilty.
    (ZOPHAR *crosses* U. S.)
    Comforters you call yourselves!
    I tell you those old women by the wall
    Who sleep there shivering have given comfort
    Greater than all of yours together:
    They gave their misery to keep me warm.

(*MUSIC.* WOMEN *rise, exit* D. R. *Except* JOLLY, *who
takes a position next to perch pole outside ring, and*
LESURE, *who stays under platform.*)

ZOPHAR. (*Crosses* D. L. C. *Kneels* L. *of* J.B. BILDAD
crosses to R. *of* J.B., *kneels;* ELIPHAZ *crosses to above*
J.B.)
    Without the fault of Adam's Fall
    We're mad men . . . all of us are mad men.
    We watch the stars (*Rises.*)
    That creep and crawl
    Like dying flies
    Across the wall
    Of night's surmise. . . .

BILDAD.
  And call . . . and call . . .
ZOPHAR.
  . . . and night replies
  And that is all.
ELIPHAZ.
  The dream replies
  And *that* is all.
BILDAD.
  The shot replies
  And that *is* all.
  (*Crosses* U. S. *to crest of ramp.* ELIPHAZ *follows to his* L.)
ZOPHAR. (*Crosses* U. S. *to* L. *of* ELIPHAZ.)
  Without the Fall
  We're mad men all.
ELIPHAZ.
  We watch the stars
  That creep and crawl
BILDAD.
  Like dying flies
  Across the wall . . .

(COMFORTERS *pause on upper ramp.*)

COMFORTERS. (*Together.*)
                    Of night! . . .
  And shriek! . . . and that is all.

(*They run out* D. R.)

NICKLES. (*Crosses above J.B.*)
  You think he'll squat there in his anguish now
  Begging the universe to love him?
  He knows now that no reasoning on earth
  Can justify the suffering he suffers.
  He knows that good is not rewarded.
  He knows that evil is not punished.
  He knows his life is meaningless. It's over.
  It's done with. Over. He'll curse God!

He'll never lift his voice again
To that deaf, unintelligible Heaven!

J.B. (*Calling out.*)
GOD . . . MY GOD! MY GOD, ANSWER ME!
I CRY OUT OF WRONG, BUT I AM NOT
   HEARD!
I CRY ALOUD, BUT THERE IS NO JUDGMENT!
THOUGH HE SLAY ME, YET WILL I TRUST
   IN HIM—
BUT I WILL MAINTAIN MY OWN WAYS BE-
   FORE HIM.

O, THAT I KNEW WHERE I MIGHT FIND HIM!
THAT I MIGHT COME EVEN TO HIS SEAT!
I WOULD ORDER MY CAUSE BEFORE HIM
(NICKLES *crosses* R. *to* R. *entrance.*)
AND FILL MY MOUTH WITH ARGUMENTS.
   BEHOLD,
I GO FORWARD BUT HE IS NOT THERE,
BACKWARD, BUT I CANNOT PERCEIVE
   HIM. . . .

(MR. ZUSS *crosses to upper edge platform.*)

DISTANT VOICE. (*Offstage.*)
WHO IS THIS THAT DARKENETH COUNSEL
BY WORDS WITHOUT KNOWLEDGE? . . .
   WHERE WAST THOU
WHEN I LAID THE FOUNDATIONS OF THE
   EARTH? . . .
WHEN THE MORNING STARS SANG TO-
   GETHER
AND ALL THE SONS OF GOD SHOUTED FOR
   JOY?

HAST THOU COMMANDED THE MORNING?
HAVE THE GATES OF DEATH BEEN OPENED
   UNTO THEE?
(NICKLES *crosses* **under platform.**)

WHERE IS THE WAY WHERE THE LIGHT
DWELLETH?
AND AS FOR THE DARKNESS, WHERE IS THE
PLACE THEREOF?

HAST THOU ENTERED INTO THE TREASURES
OF THE SNOW?

BY WHAT WAY IS THE LIGHT PARTED
WHICH SCATTERETH THE EAST WIND UPON
THE EARTH?

CAN'ST THOU BIND THE SWEET INFLUENCES
OF THE PLEIADES?

HAST THOU GIVEN THE HORSE STRENGTH?
HAST THOU CLOTHED HIS NECK WITH
THUNDER?
HE SAITH AMONG THE TRUMPETS, HA, HA;
HE SMELLETH THE BATTLE AFAR OFF,
THE THUNDER OF THE CAPTAINS AND THE
SHOUTING.

DOTH THE EAGLE MOUNT UP AT THY COM-
MAND?
(LESURE *rises: crosses to* JOLLY.)

HER EYES BEHOLD AFAR OFF.
HER YOUNG ONES ALSO SUCK UP BLOOD:
AND WHERE THE SLAIN ARE, THERE IS
SHE. . . .
JOLLY.
Mother! Mother! Mother! What was
That?
LESURE. (*Drawing* JOLLY *off* D. R.)
        The wind, child. Only the wind.
    Only the wind.
JOLLY.
                There was a word.

LESURE.
  You heard the thunder in the wind.
JOLLY.
  Under the wind, there was a word.

(*They go out,* D. R.)

DISTANT VOICE. (*Offstage.*)
  HE THAT REPROVETH GOD, LET HIM AN-
    SWER IT!
J.B.
  BEHOLD, I AM VILE: WHAT SHALL I ANSWER
    THEE?
  I WILL LAY MINE HAND UPON MY MOUTH.
DISTANT VOICE. (J.B. *cowers lower and lower under
the words.*)
  GIRD UP THY LOINS LIKE A MAN.
  I WILL DEMAND OF THEE, AND DECLARE
    THOU UNTO ME.

  WILT THOU DISANNUL MY JUDGMENT?

  WILT THOU CONDEMN
  ME THAT THOU MAYST BE RIGHTEOUS?

  HAST THOU AN ARM LIKE GOD? OR CANST
    THOU
  THUNDER WITH A VOICE LIKE HIM?

  DECK THYSELF NOW WITH MAJESTY AND
    EXCELLENCY
  AND ARRAY THYSELF WITH GLORY AND
    BEAUTY . . .
  THEN WILL I ALSO CONFESS UNTO THEE
  THAT THINE OWN RIGHT HAND CAN SAVE
    THEE.

(MR. ZUSS *crosses to front and* C. *of platform.* J.B.
*slowly lifts his head, looks at his hand—lifted from be-
neath covering.* TRUMPET, *off.*)

J.B.
    I KNOW THAT THOU CANST DO EVERY-
        THING . . .
    AND THAT NO THOUGHT CAN BE WITH-
        HOLDEN FROM THEE.
    WHEREFORE HAVE I UTTERED THAT I UN-
        DERSTAND NOT,
    THINGS TOO WONDERFUL FOR ME . . .
        WHICH I UNDERSTOOD
    NOT. HEAR, I BESEECH THEE, AND I WILL
        SPEAK.
    I HAVE HEARD OF THEE BY THE HEARING
        OF THE EAR
    (Mr. Zuss *stretches his open hands to* J.B.)
    BUT NOW MINE EYE SEETH THEE,
                                    WHEREFORE
    I ABHOR MYSELF AND REPENT.

(*A long silence.*)

Nickles. (*Emerging from beneath platform.*)
    Well, that's that!
Mr. Zuss.
                    That's *that.*
Nickles.
    You win.
Mr. Zuss.
                Of course I win. I told you.
Nickles. (*Removing Devil's garb.*)
    Pious, contemptible, goddam sheep!
    (*Flings garb upstage.*)
    Repenting! And for what? For asking
    Reasons of the universe! For asking *why!*
Mr. Zuss. (*Exalted.*)
    He had heard of God, and now he saw him.
    Planets and Pleiades and eagles,
    Screaming horses, scales of light,
    Last Orion, least sea shell,
    The wonder and the mystery of the universe,
    Beauty beyond the feel of fingers,

Marvel beyond the maze of mind,
The whole creation: Searchless power
Burning on the hearth of stars. . . .

NICKLES.
Where did I put that *popcorn* . . . ?

(*In the darkness, under the platform* R., NICKLES *straps
on his tray of popcorn.* MR. ZUSS *stands above, lost in
the ecstasy of his triumph. Unseen by either,* J.B. *lifts
his face from the earth, his eyes on the audience. His
voice is a whisper at first in which the great words he has
heard return to his mouth with the sour of mortality on
them.*)

J.B.
Hast thou an Arm . . . ?
                        like God . . . ?
                        and can'st thou . . . ?

MR. ZUSS.
His was the true repentance, wasn't it?

J.B. (*He has raised himself a little more on his knees.*)
Deck thyself now . . .
                    with Majesty . . .
                        and Excellency . . .

MR. ZUSS.
True surrender! To the fear of God!
Not to the love: the fear!

J.B.
                    Deck thyself!
Then will I also confess unto thee
That thine own . . . right . . . hand . . .
(*He lifts his scorched right hand before his eyes*)
                        can *save* thee!

(NICKLES *crosses to ramp outside* R. *entrance of ring.*)

MR. ZUSS.
Comfort, you see, is not a changing fashion.
Comfort is one and always the same

For every human heart. We have no
Comfort but the fear of God.
NICKLES.
He feared, my friend. Why not? Why wouldn't he? . . .
J.B.
Wherefore . . .
            Wherefore . . .
                    I abhor myself . . .
                            and repent!

NICKLES.
God with all those stars and stallions:
Throwing the whole creation at him!
Job with little children's bones. . . .
Let's not talk about those children!
MR. ZUSS. (*Triumphantly.*)
He feared God and he repented!
NICKLES.
The choice is swallowing this swill of world
Or vomiting in the trough. Job swallowed it.
That's God's triumph—that he swallowed it.
MR. ZUSS. (*Shocked at last.*)
Is God to be forgiven?
NICKLES. (*A long, insolent look.*)
            Isn't He?

(NICKLES *turns his back on* MR. ZUSS; *crosses to the
aisle by which he entered.*)

MR. ZUSS. (*Choking with anger.*)
That's not the end.
NICKLES.
            Why not? You win.
You've made your bow. You want another?
MR. ZUSS. (*Shouting angrily after him.*)
You know as well as I there's more.
There's always one more scene no matter
Who plays Job or when.
(NICKLES *keeps on up the aisles.*)
                    You're running
Out! You haven't got the guts

To play your part through.
(NICKLES *ad libs "Ah—go ——!"*)
                                        You're no actor!
You're a popcorn peddler to the heart!
NICKLES. (*Stung in his professional pride; returning to
below ring—on lower ramp.*)
    What other scene?
MR. ZUSS.

                            The scene that ends it.
God restores him at the end.
NICKLES.
    God restores us all. That's normal.
    That's God's mercy to mankind.
    We never asked Him to be born.
    We never chose the lives we die of.
    They beat our rumps to make us breathe.
    But God, if we have suffered patiently,
    Borne it in silence, stood the stench,
    (*He slaps the floor of the ring.*)
    Rewards us. Gives our dirty souls back.
MR. ZUSS.
    God restores him *here*. On *earth*.
    Gives him all he ever had and
    More.
NICKLES. (*Starting out again.*)
            Sure! His wife! His children!
MR. ZUSS.
    He gets his wife back and the children . . .
    Follow in nature's course.
NICKLES. (*Stopped short in the aisle: turning.*)
                            You're lying.
MR. ZUSS.
    I'm not lying.
NICKLES. (*Passionately. Races back to ramp* D. R. *of
ring.*)
                    I say you're lying.
MR. ZUSS.
    Why should I lie? It's in the Book.

NICKLES.

    Wife back! *Wife!* He wouldn't touch her.
    He wouldn't take her with a glove.
    After all that filth and blood and
    Fury to begin again!
    After life like his to take
    The seed up of the sad creation
    Planting the hopeful world again. . . .
    He can't.
        He won't.
            He wouldn't touch her.

MR. ZUSS.

    He does though.

NICKLES.

            Live his life again?
    Not even the most ignorant, obstinate,
    Stupid or degraded man
    This filthy planet ever farrowed,
    Offered the opportunity to live
    His bodily life twice over, would accept it—
    Least of all Job, poor trampled bastard!
    It can't be borne twice over!
                Can't be!
    (*Slaps platform, under* MR. ZUSS' *feet.*)

MR. ZUSS.

    It is though. Time and again it is.
    Every blessed generation.
    (*Relishing his triumph; laying it on.*)
    Time and again!
            Time and again!

(J.B. *has struggled to his knees. Now, by an almost in-
tolerable effort, he is on his feet.* NICKLES *crosses a step,
watching* J.B.)

J.B.

    Repent? For crying out? For suffering?

(NICKLES *and* MR. ZUSS *hear him at last.*)

Mr. Zuss.

Did you hear that?

Nickles. (*Crosses to* r. *entrance of ring.*)

I did.

J.B.

Must I be

Dumb because my mouth is mortal?—
Blind because my eyes will one day
Close forever? Is that my wickedness—
That I am weak?

(*He takes off his shawl of rags.*)

Nickles. (*Mocking* Mr. Zuss.)

Time and again!

J.B.

Must my breath, my breathing, be forgiven me?

Nickles. (*He removes the popcorn tray and stows it under the platform* r.)

Time and again, eh? J.B.!

(*Entering ring.*)

J.B.!

J.B.

Let me alone.

(J.B. *takes some of his rags and his shawl, crosses to* u. l. *side of ring, and throws them over the ring-wall.*)

Nickles.

It's me.

I'm not the Father. I'm the . . . Friend.

J.B. (*Crosses back to his remaining rags.*)

I have no friend.

Nickles.

O, come off it.

You don't have to act with me.

(J.B. *is silent.*)

O.K. Carry on.

All I wanted was to help.

Professional counsel you might call it.

(J.B. *is silent—on his knees.*)

Of course you know how all this ends?

(J.B. *is silent.*)
I wondered how you'd play the end.
J.B.
What end is there?
NICKLES. (*Takes rags from* J.B., *throws them out of the ring,* U. L., *returns to* J.B.)

                You don't know?
Why should I tell you when you know?
What is the worst thing you can think of?
J.B.
I have asked for death. Begged for it. Prayed for it.
NICKLES.
Then the worst thing can't be death.
(J.B. *stares at him.*)
He gives it back to you.
J.B.

                What back?

NICKLES.

                      Everything.

Everything He ever took—
Wife, health, children . . . everything.
J.B. (*Rises.*)
I have no wife.
NICKLES.

            He gives her back to you.
J.B. (*Crosses* D. L. *in ring.*)
I have no children.
NICKLES.

            You'll have better ones.

J.B.
My skin is . . .

(*He breaks off.*)

NICKLES.

           O, come on. I know the
Look of greasepaint!
J.B. (*Takes off coat, stares at his arms.*)

           . . . whole! It's healed!
(*He repeats the word as* NICKLES *goes on.*)

NICKLES. (*Heavily ironic—grabbing J.B.'s coat.*)
You see? You see what I mean? What he plans for
   you?
(SARAH *appears at the edge of light* D. R., *moving
slowly toward the ring on upper ramp, a little green
branch in her fingers.* NICKLES *sees her. His voice
rises.*)
Tell me how you'll play the end—
Any man was screwed as Job was. . . .
(*He moves between* J.B. *and* SARAH.)
I'll tell you how to play it! Listen!
Think of all the mucked up millions
Since this buggered world began
Said No! said Thank you! took a rope's end.
Took a window for a door,
Swallowed something, gagged on something. . . .
(J.B. *lifts his head listening, but not to* NICKLES.)
Not one of them had known what you know.
Not one had learned *Job's* truth.

(*He casts* J.B.'s *coat out of the ring* U. L. SARAH *stands
outside upper entrance to the ring.*)

J.B.
                                    There's someone . . .
NICKLES. (*Backs to upper entrance of the ring.*)
Job won't take it. Job won't touch it.
J.B.
There's someone standing at the door.
NICKLES.
Job won't take it! Job won't touch it!
Job will . . .
(*He looks up at* MR. ZUSS, *dashes* R. *at him up the
stair.*)
            . . . fling it in God's face
With half his guts to make it spatter.
He'd rather suffocate in dung,
Drown in ordure . . .
(*He attempts to scale the stair to the high perch; col-
lapses.*)

                          Suffocate in dung,
Drown in ordure. . . .

(MR. ZUSS *flings off his robe in a gesture of triumph and
strides down the stair, his face shining. He enters the
ring where* J.B. *and* SARAH *stand opposite each other, she
looking up at him, half tender, half afraid; he, his mouth
grim, turned away.*)

MR. ZUSS. (*Crosses to* J.B. *A bit above.*)
    Job! You've answered him!
J.B.
    Let me alone. 1 am alone.
    I'll sweat it out alone.
MR. ZUSS.
                              You've found
    The answer at the end! You've answered him!
    We take what God has sent—the Godsend.
    (*A gesture toward* SARAH. J.B. *is silent.*)
    There is no resolution of the mystery
    Of unintelligible suffering but the dumb
    Bowed head that makes injustice just
    By yielding to the Will that willed it—
    Yielding to the Will that willed
    A world where there can be injustice.
    (*Crosses* R. C. *toward* SARAH.)
    You've learned that now. You've bowed your head.
    (J.B. *is silent.* SARAH *takes a tentative step toward
    him.*)
    The end is the acceptance of the end.
    We take what God has willed.
J.B. (*Crosses to* MR. ZUSS. *Savagely.*)
                                    I will not
    Duck my head again to thunder—
    That bullwhip crackling at my ears!—although
    He kill me with it. I must know.

(NICKLES *has risen and is making his way slowly down
the stair.*)

MR. ZUSS. (*Astonished. He could not have heard what he has heard.*)

    We have no *peace* but in obedience.

    Our peace is acquiescence in the Will of God.

J.B.

    I'll find a foothold somewhere *knowing*.

    (*Crosses* R. *to* SARAH. NICKLES *crosses down platform and down steps. To* NICKLES.)

    Life is a filthy farce, you say,

    And nothing but a bloody stage

    Can bring the curtain down and men

    Must have ironic hearts and perish

    Laughing. . . .

    (MR. ZUSS *crosses* D. L.)

               Well, *I* will not laugh!

    (*He swings on* MR. ZUSS.)

    And neither will I weep among

    The obedient who lie down to die

    In meek relinquishment protesting

    Nothing, questioning nothing, asking

    Nothing but to rise again and

                      bow!

    Neither the bowing nor the blood

    Will make an end for me now!

                    Neither the

    Yes in ignorance . . .

                  the No in spite. . . .

    Neither of them!

    (MR. ZUSS *exits ring to ramp at* L.)

               Neither of them!

    (NICKLES *crosses* D. *to* R. *ramp.*)

    Sarah!

          Why have you come back again?

SARAH. (*Confused, holding out the small green branch like a child.*)

    Look, Job.

          The first few leaves . . .

                    Not leaves though—

    Petals. I found it in the ashes growing

Green as though it did not know . . .
All that's left there now is ashes. . . .
Mountains of ashes, shattered glass,
Glittering cliffs of glass all shattered
Steeper than a cat could climb
If there were cats still. . . .

J.B.

Why?

SARAH.

I broke the
Branch to strip the leaves off.
Petals
(*Fastens branch to pole at* R. C., *under perch.*)
Again!
But they so clung to it!

J.B.

Curse
God and die! You said that to me.

SARAH.

Yes. You wanted justice, didn't you?

J.B.

Cry for justice and the stars
Will stare until your eyes sting! Weep,
Enormous winds will thrash the water!

SARAH.

Cry in sleep for your lost children,
Snow will fall . . .

snow will fall.

J.B.

You left me, Sarah.

SARAH.

Yes, I left you.
I thought there was a way away.
Out of the world. Out of the world.
Water under bridges opens
Closing and the companion stars
Still float there afterwards. I thought the door
Opened into closing water.

J.B.
  Sarah!
SARAH.
          Oh, I never could.
  I never could. Even this—
  Even the green leaf on the branch—could stop me.
J.B.
  Why have you come back again?
SARAH. (*Kneels* C. *She has found a stub of candle in her pocket.*)
  Because I love you.
J.B.
                    Because you love me!
  The one thing certain in this hurtful world
  Is love's inevitable heartbreak.
  What's the future but the past to come
  Over and over, love and loss,
  What's loved most lost most.

(SARAH *has moved into the rubble of the ring. She kneels, setting things to rights. Her mind is on her task, not on J.B.'s words.*)

SARAH.
                    I know that, Job.
J.B.
  Nothing is certain but the loss of love.
  And yet . . . you say you love me!
SARAH.
                              Yes.
J.B.
  The stones in those dead streets would crack
  With terrible indecent laughter
  Hearing *you* and *me* say love!
SARAH.
  I have no light to light the candle.
J.B. (*Violently.*)
  You have our love to light it with!
  Blow on the coal of the heart, poor Sarah.
SARAH.
  Blow on the coal of the heart . . . ?

J.B.
The candles in churches are out.
The lights have gone out in the sky!

SARAH.
The candles in churches are out.
The lights have gone out in the sky.
Blow on the coal of the heart
And we'll see by and by. . . .

                        we'll see where we are.

We'll know. We'll know.

J.B. (*Slowly, with difficulty, the hard words said at last.*)
                We can never *know*.

He answered me like the stillness of a star
That silences us asking.

             No, Sarah, no:

(*Kneels beside her.*)
We *are* and that is all our answer.
We are and what we are can suffer.
But . . .

       what suffers loves.

              And love

Will live its suffering again,
Risk its own defeat again,
Endure the loss of everything again
And yet again and yet again
In doubt, in dread, in ignorance, unanswered,
Over and over, with the dark before,
The dark behind it . . . and still live . . . still love.

(**J.B.** *strikes match, touches* **SARAH'S** *cheek with his hand.*)

(GAUZE CURTAIN DROPS. *MUSIC. LIGHTS FADE OUT.*)

THE PLAY IS ENDED

In the darkness, the gauze curtain rises.
Lights come up for calls:
1. (L. to R.) MR. ZUSS, J.B., SARAH, NICKLES. They
   bow, walk D. S., bow, exit U. L.
2. ROUSTABOUTS and PROP WOMEN enter D. R., bow,
   move U. S. (ROUSTABOUTS to D. R.)
3. CHILDREN enter from L., bow, cross U. S. C. and
   around to outside L. of ring.
4. GIRL enters D. R., followed by MURPHY, ADAMS, LE-
   SURE. GIRL steps into ring at R.; WOMEN stand on
   D. R. ramp. Bow. They move to places U. R. C. outside
   ring.
5. BILDAD, ELIPHAZ, ZOPHAR enter L., cross to C., bow.
   Cross U. R. C. to above ring at R.
6. ZUSS, J.B., SARAH and NICKLES enter over stairs,
   U. S. C. Come D. C. Bow. They exit L.

(WORK LIGHTS. CALLIOPE MUSIC. HOUSE
LIGHTS.)

(*Company exits*, R. *and* L.)

J.B.

PROPERTY LIST

ON STAGE

On wardrobe-platform section:

On floor:

Wooden box for MR. ZUSS to sit on.

Satan and Godmasks behind box.

In S. L. compartment:

On pipe:

1 grey robe—prop costume.

On hook:

Grey sports coat—1ST REPORTER.

In pocket—2 cigarettes and lighter.

Felt hat with press card.

On floor:

Police raincoat with badge—1ST POLICEMAN.

Felt hat on raincoat—1ST REPORTER.

Overseas cap—1ST SOLDIER.

In S. R. compartment:

On pipe:

MR. ZUSS's robe—NICKLES' sash on floor under it.

1 grey robe—prop costume.

On hook:

Brown sports coat—2ND REPORTER.

In pocket—spiral pad and pencil.

Overseas cap—2D SOLDIER.

On floor:

Police raincoat with badge—2D POLICEMAN.

Behind U. S. ramp on stage floor—coil of ¾" rope.

Up L. on stage floor behind raised circus banners—9 stools:

Two for 2D ROUSTABOUT to place stage R.

Seven for PROP WOMEN to place at family table.

Off L. in "Family" entrance:

Small table.

Folded dust cover.
Prop basket:
    6 goblets.
    2 wine glasses.
Tablecloth.
Centerpiece for table.
On prop table off s. l.:
    Turkey on platter—1st Maid.
    Carving knife and fork—2d Maid.
    Knife sharpener—1st Maid.
    Decanter and 4 old-fashioned glasses—J.B.
    Money—Miss Mabel (The Girl).
    Camera—Prop Woman.
    Bibs—Jonathan and Rebecca.
    Cigar and matches—J.B.
    Crocheting—Sarah.
    Bundles of rags—Mrs. Murphy and Mrs. Adams.
    "Daily News"—Mrs. Murphy.
    Bunch of balloons—Mr. Zuss.
    Popcorn tray—Nickles.
    False noses—Mr. Zuss and Nickles.
    Twist bell—Stage Manager.
On prop table off s. r.:
    Parasol, wrapped—2d Policeman.
    Police notebook and pencil—1st Policeman.
    Pocket knife—2d Policeman.
    1 pipe and tobacco—Bildad.
    Cigars—1st Roustabout and Zophar.
    Newspaper; headline: WAR ENDS—V-J Soldier.
    Crutch—V-J Soldier.
    Army canteen and belt—2d Defense Officer.
    Flashlight—1st Defense Officer.
    Thunderdrum and drumstick—Stage Manager.
In perch, over the stage—large drumstick for Mr. Zuss.

SPOON RIVER ANTHOLOGY

CHARLES AIDMAN

Conceived from EDGAR LEE MASTERS'
'Spoon River Anthology'

3 men, 2 women—A stage

Via musical interludes, we are introduced in a cemetery to the ghosts of those who were inhabitants of this town, and whose secrets have gone with them to the grave. There are 60-odd characterizations and vignettes in this constantly interesting entertainment, offering an amazingly varied array of roles and impersonations, from young lovers and preachers and teachers, to the funny chronicle of the poor mixed-up Jew who ends up in the wrong cemetery. Both the sordid and the humorous sides of life are portrayed, with fetching ballads, and the free verse form of Masters. "A dramatic presentation reduced to its simplest terms . . . moving and beautiful . . . an evening of astonishing stirring emotional satisfaction."—*N. Y. Post.* "A glowing theatre experience . . . a brooding and loving American folk poem brought to life on a stage."—*N. Y. Times.* "Vivid . . . quite an inspiration. . . . A decided novelty. . . . It has punch and humor and bitterness, and often it stabs the heart."—*N. Y. Daily News.* "Warm, radiant, poetic. . . . A compelling experience in the theatre."—*N. Y. Journal-American.* "A procession of unforgettable men and women, and a powerful evocation of life."—*N. Y. World-Telegram & Sun.*

(Royalty, $50–$25)

DAVID and LISA

By JAMES REACH

Adapted from the book by THEODORE ISAAC RUBIN, and the screenplay by ELEANOR PERRY

11 men, 11 women

The production is extremely simple; it is played against drapes and uses a minimum of props. The award-winning motion picture, *David and Lisa,* has now been adapted for the stage with the utmost fidelity to its illustrious prototype. It retells, by use of the most modern stage techniques, the strange, appealing and utterly fascinating story of the two mentally-disturbed adolescents: David, only son of wealthy parents, over-protected by a dominating mother, who is tortured by his mania against being touched; and Lisa, the waif who has never known parental love, who has developed a split personality and is in effect two different girls, one of whom will speak only in childish rhymes and insists upon being spoken to in the same manner. The play follows them during the course of one term at Berkley School, where they have come under the sympathetic and understanding guidance of psychiatrist Alan Swinford and his staff; follows them through exhilarating progress and depressing retrogression; follows them—and their fellow students: Carlos, the street urchin; the over-romantic Kate; stout Sandra, and others—with laughter and heartbreak and suspense.

(Royalty $35–$25)

FAVORITE BROADWAY DRAMAS
from
SAMUEL FRENCH, INC.

ALL THE WAY HOME – THE AMEN CORNER –
AMERICAN BUFFALO – ANASTASIA – ANGEL
STREET – BECKET – THE BELLE OF AMHERST –
BUTLEY – COLD STORAGE – COME BACK, LITTLE
SHEBA – A DAY IN THE DEATH OF JOE EGG –
A DELICATE BALANCE – THE DESPERATE HOURS
– THE ELEPHANT MAN – EQUUS – FORTUNE AND
MEN'S EYES – A HATFUL OF RAIN – THE
HOMECOMING – J.B. – KENNEDY'S CHILDREN –
LOOK HOMEWARD, ANGEL – A MAN FOR ALL
SEASONS – THE MIRACLE WORKER – A MOON FOR
THE MISBEGOTTEN – NO PLACE TO BE SOMEBODY
– ONE FLEW OVER THE CUCKOO'S NEXT – OUR
TOWN – A RAISIN IN THE SUN – THE RIVER
NIGER – THE SHADOW BOX – SIX CHARACTERS
IN SEARCH OF AN AUTHOR – STICKS AND BONES –
THE SUBJECT WAS ROSES – TEA AND SYMPATHY –
THE VISIT – WINGS

For descriptions of all our plays, consult our Basic Catalogue of Plays

Other Publications for Your Interest

THE DRESSER
(LITTLE THEATRE—DRAMA)

By RONALD HARWOOD

10 men, 3 women—Complete Interior

Sir, the last of the great, but dying, breed of English actor/managers, is in a very bad way tonight. As his dresser tries valiantly to prepare him to go on stage as King Lear, Sir is having great difficulty remembering who and where he is, let alone Lear's lines. With a Herculean effort on the part of Norman, the dresser, Sir finally does make it on stage, and through the performance—no thanks to the bombs of the *Luftwaffe*, which are falling all around the theatre (the play takes place back stage on an English provincial theatre during an air raid during World War II). It is to be Sir's last performance, though; for backstage in his dressing room after the performance, the worn out old trouper dies—leaving his company—and, in particular, his loyal dresser—alone with their loneliness. "A stirring evening . . . burns with a love of the theater that conquers all . . . perfectly observed, devilishly entertaining backstage lore."—N.Y. Times. "Sheer wonderful theatricality . . . I think you'll love it as much as I did."— N.Y. Daily News. "Enthralling, funny and touching. Lovingly delineated dramatic portraits . . . Almost any actor would jump at them."—N.Y. Post. "A wonderfully affectionate and intelligent play about the theatre."—The Guardian, London.

(For Future Release. Royalty, $60-$40, when available.)

EQUUS
(LITTLE THEATRE—MORALITY)

By PETER SHAFFER

5 men, 4 women, 6 actors to play horses—Basic setting

Martin Dysart, a psychiatrist, is confronted with Alan Strang, a boy who has blinded six horses. To the owner of the horses the horror is simple: he was unlucky enough to employ 'a loony'. To the boy's parents it is a hideous mystery: Alan had always adored horses, and although Dora Strang may have been a slightly overindulgent mother and Frank Strang a slightly tetchy father, they both loved their son. To Dysart it is a psychological puzzle to be untangled and pain to be alleviated . . . or rather, given his profession, that is what it ought to be. As it turns out, it is something far more complex and disturbing: a confrontation with himself as well as with Alan, in which he comes to an inescapable view of man's need to worship and the distortions forced on that need by "civilized" society. Since this is a story of discovery, the reader's excitement would be diminished by a detailed account of its development. "The closest I have seen a contemporary play come to reanimating the spirit of mystery that makes the stage a place of breathless discovery rather than a classroom for rational demonstration. Mr. Shaffer may have been trying for just such iconography—a portrait of the drives that lead men to crucify themselves—there. Here I think he's found it."—Walter Kerr, N.Y. Times.

(Royalty, $50-$35.)

Other Publications for Your Interest

THE ROYAL HUNT OF THE SUN
(ALL GROUPS—HISTORY)
By PETER SHAFFER

22 men, 2 women—Cyc, drops, inset

The expedition of the Spanish under Pizzaro to the land of the Incas told in dazzling spectacle and moral chiaroscuro. After general absolution for any crimes they may commit against the pagan Incas, the conquerors set forth upon the sea. The Inca god is a sun god, ruler of the riches and people of Peru, and thought to be immortal. But the Spaniards have come in conquest rather than in reverence. There is a misunderstanding, confusion, and a slaughter in which the Spaniards kill 3000 unarmed and take the sun god captive. The ransom is 9000 pounds of gold. The avaricious Spaniards mutiny, try the sun god in kangaroo court, and then garrot him. He does not revive, and the Incas behold their dead god. "High intelligence and bold, imaginative reach . . . It has elements of the masque (and) pageant, soaring passages that recall the stage to its lofty enterprise, and a theme of enduring significance."—N.Y. Times. "Greatest play of our generation."—London Daily Mail.

(Royalty, $50–$25.)

BLACK COMEDY
(LITTLE THEATRE—FARCE)
By PETER SHAFFER

5 men, 3 women—Interior

Taking a page from the Chinese theatre, this farce opens on a dark stage (which is light to the characters), then blows a fuse throwing them all in the dark (which is light to the audience), and ends with lights reconnected (i.e., with a dark stage). What we see in the "dark" is this: A girl bringing her wealthy father to meet her fiance, an improvident sculptor, and to impress him, the sculptor has both invited a wealthy art patron and stolen the fine furniture from the apartment next door for his bare pad. Not only have the lights gone out, but everything else turns cockeyed—the neighbor returns too soon, the art patron is mistaken for an electrician, and a former flame pixies the proceedings from the bedroom. "Grand slapstick . . . Jolted me with laughter, and I was sorry indeed when the stage went dark and farce ended."—N.Y. Daily News. "A remarkably ingenious farce."—Wall Street Journal. "A truly hilarious and original farce . . . farcial situations and amusing characters that keep the hilarity spinning festively in the air."—N.Y. Post. "An evening with this uproarious play is like the rediscovery of laughter."—N.Y. World Journal Tribune. One of the biggest hits of the season and a perfect play for Little Theatre and College groups.

(Royalty, $50–$25.)

Other Publications for Your Interest

PAST TENSE
(LITTLE THEATRE—DRAMA)

By JACK ZEMAN

1 man, 1 woman, 2 optional men—Interior

This compelling new play is about the breakup of a marriage. It is set on the day Emily and Ralphy Michaelson, a prosperous middle-aged couple, break off a union of 27 years. As they confront each other in their packed-up living room one final time, they alternately taunt and caress one another. She has never 'forgiven him for a petty infidelity of years ago. He has never forgiven her for her inability to express grief over the long-ago accidental death of their youngest child. In a series of flashbacks, Mr. Zeman dredges up the pivotal events of his characters' lives. Barbara Feldon and Laurence Luckinbill starred on Broadway in this at times humorous, and ultimately very moving play by a talented new playwright. " . . . rich in theatrical devices, sassy talk and promising themes."—N.Y. Times. "There is no doubt that Zeman can write. His backbiting, backlashing dialogue has considerable gusto—it belts out with a most impressively muscular vigor and intellectual vivacity."—N.Y. Post.

(Royalty, $50–$35)

SCENES AND REVELATIONS
(ALL GROUPS—DRAMA)

By ELAN GARONZIK

3 men, 4 women—Platform set

Set in 1894 at the height of America's westward movement, the play portrays the lives of four Pennsylvania sisters who decide not to move west, but to England. It opens with the sisters prepared to leave their farm and birthplace forever. Then a series of lyrical flashbacks dramatize the tender and frustrating romances of the women. Rebecca, the youngest, marries and moves west to Nebraska, only to find she is ill-prepared for pioneer life. Millie, a bohemian artist, falls in love with the farm boy next door; when he marries a woman without Millie's worldly aspirations, she is crushed. Charlotte, a nurse, is rejected by her doctor on religious principles. Only Helena, the eldest, has the promise of a bright and bold life in California with Samuel, the farm's manager. However, Rebecca's tragic return east moves the sisters to unite for the promise of a better life in England. "A deeply human play . . . a rocket to the moon of imagination," Claudia Cassidy—WFMT, Chicago. "Humanly full . . . glimmers with revelation," Elliott—Chicago Sun-Times. "The play is a beauty," Sharp—WWD. "A deep understanding of women and their relationships with men," Barnes—New York Post.

(Royalty, $50–$35.)